United States Government Accountability Office

Report to Congressional Addressees

I0448230

December 2013

DODD-FRANK REGULATIONS

Agencies Conducted Regulatory Analyses and Coordinated but Could Benefit from Additional Guidance on Major Rules

DODD-FRANK REGULATIONS

Agencies Conducted Regulatory Analyses and Coordinated but Could Benefit from Additional Guidance on Major Rules

Highlights of GAO-14-67, a report to congressional addressees

Why GAO Did This Study

The 2010 Dodd-Frank Act requires or authorizes various federal agencies to issue hundreds of rules to implement reforms intended to strengthen the financial services industry. As amended by Public Law No. 112-10, the act also mandates that GAO annually study financial services regulations. This report examines (1) the regulatory analyses agencies conducted in their Dodd-Frank rulemakings; (2) interagency coordination on such rulemakings and by CFPB in its supervision activities; and (3) the possible impact of selected Dodd-Frank provisions and related rules and agency plans to assess Dodd-Frank Act rules retrospectively. GAO identified and reviewed 70 Dodd-Frank rules that became effective from July 24, 2012, through July 22, 2013, to determine whether the required regulatory analyses and coordination were conducted; examined CFPB's policies, procedures, and other materials; developed indicators on the impact of the act's systemic risk-related provisions and rules; conducted a regression analysis to assess the act's impact on large bank holding companies; and interviewed federal financial regulators and officials from the U.S. Department of the Treasury, the Financial Stability Oversight Council, and OMB.

What GAO Recommends

GAO recommends that OMB issue guidance to help standardize CRA processes. OMB disagreed such guidance is needed, in part because GAO did not identify inconsistencies in major rule designations. GAO maintains that the identified process inconsistencies could lead to differing designations under CRA, and its recommendation helps ensure consistency in designating major rules.

View GAO-14-67. For more information, contact A. Nicole Clowers at (202) 512-8678 or clowersa@gao.gov.

What GAO Found

Federal agencies conducted the required regulatory analyses for all rules issued pursuant to the Dodd-Frank Wall Street Reform and Consumer Protection Act (Dodd-Frank Act) that GAO identified and reviewed. However, the Office of Management and Budget (OMB), in coordination with the agencies, may not be consistently determining which rules are considered major rules under the Congressional Review Act (CRA). Under the act, Congress is allowed to review major rules before they become effective. The act outlines criteria for determining whether a rule is major, such as whether it will result in an annual effect on the economy of $100 million or more. OMB is responsible for determining which rules are major under CRA but relies on agency analyses to help make the determination. OMB guidance does not address whether independent agencies should submit all rules for review or how they should apply major rule criteria. GAO found that some independent agencies submitted all their rules to OMB, but others did not. GAO also found inconsistencies in how these agencies applied the CRA criteria. For example, GAO found rules issued by different agencies that had similar economic impacts but were not similarly classified as major. These issues raise the risk of some rules not being properly classified as major, limiting Congress's ability to review these rules before they become effective.

Federal regulators coordinated on 49 rulemakings pursuant to the Dodd-Frank Act or voluntarily. As required by the act, the Consumer Financial Protection Bureau (CFPB) established a framework to coordinate its supervision activities with prudential regulators and is establishing a similar framework to coordinate with state regulators. In May 2012, CFPB and prudential regulators entered into an agreement that specifies how they plan to meet the act's coordination requirements for the supervision of large banks (i.e., more than $10 billion in assets). CFPB has entered into similar agreements with state regulators to coordinate examinations of banks and nonbank financial entities.

The Dodd-Frank Act has not been fully implemented and its full impact remains uncertain. Using recently released data, GAO updated its prior report's indicators monitoring certain risk characteristics of large U.S. bank holding companies. Although changes in the indicators are not evidence of causal links to the act's provisions, some indicators suggest these companies, on average, have decreased their leverage and enhanced their liquidity since the act's passage. Moreover, GAO's updated regression analysis suggests that the act continued to have little effect on the funding costs of large U.S. bank holding companies but may have helped improve their safety and soundness. Based on its analysis of the act and market data, GAO also developed new indicators for this report to monitor the extent to which certain of the act's swap reforms are associated with their intended outcomes. These indicators establish baselines for measuring future changes. Finally, GAO examined federal financial regulators' plans to conduct retrospective reviews of their Dodd-Frank rules. Executive Order 13,579 asks independent agencies, including federal financial regulators, to develop plans to conduct retrospective reviews of existing rules that may be excessively burdensome or costly. Regulators have varied in their approaches and progress in developing and implementing such plans. Given the importance of such reviews, GAO recommended in 2011 that the regulators determine how they will measure the impact of Dodd-Frank regulations in their plans, but they have not done so to date. GAO maintains that doing so would position the regulators to make their future retrospective reviews as robust as possible.

_____ **United States Government Accountability Office**

Contents

Letter		1
	Background	6
	Agencies Conducted Required Regulatory Analyses but May Not Be Identifying All Major Rules	13
	Regulators Continue to Coordinate on Rulemakings	20
	Impacts of the Dodd-Frank Act Are Uncertain, and Regulators Are Developing Plans to Review Rules Retrospectively	34
	Conclusions	60
	Recommendations for Executive Action	60
	Agency Comments and Our Evaluation	61

Appendix I	Objectives, Scope, and Methodology	67

Appendix II	Dodd-Frank Rules Effective as of July 22, 2013	72

Appendix III	Dodd-Frank Rules Classified as Major, Final as of July 22, 2013	87

Appendix IV	Interagency Coordination for Dodd-Frank Rules Effective on July 24, 2012, through July 22, 2013	89

Appendix V	Summary of Rulemakings Related to Selected Dodd-Frank Provisions Applicable to Systemically Important Financial Institutions	98

Appendix VI	Trends in GAO Indicators for Bank SIFIs	103

Appendix VII	Econometric Analyses of the Impact of Enhanced Regulation and Oversight on SIFIs	117

Appendix VIII	Dodd-Frank Rules Implementing Central Clearing, Capital, and Margin Swap Reforms	126
Appendix IX	Comments from the Financial Stability Oversight Council	128
Appendix X	Comments from the National Credit Union Administration	130
Appendix XI	GAO Contact and Acknowledgments	131

Tables

Table 1: Prudential Regulators and Their Basic Functions — 7
Table 2: Summary of Trends in Indicators for Bank SIFIs, from Third Quarter 2010 through Second Quarter 2013 — 38
Table 3: Estimated Changes in U.S. Bank SIFIs' Funding Costs and Measures of Safety and Soundness Associated with the Dodd-Frank Act, from Third Quarter 2010 through Second Quarter 2013 — 41
Table 4: Dodd-Frank Rules Effective from July 24, 2012, through July 22, 2013 — 72
Table 5: Dodd-Frank Rules Effective from July 22, 2011, through July 23, 2012 — 77
Table 6: Dodd-Frank Rules Effective as of July 21, 2011 — 84
Table 7: Dodd-Frank Rules Classified as Major, Final as of July 22, 2013 — 87
Table 8: Evidence of Interagency Coordination in Dodd-Frank Regulations Effective July 24, 2012, through July 22, 2013 — 89
Table 9: Rulemakings Implementing Selected Dodd-Frank Provisions Applicable to Systemically Important Financial Institutions and Their Status as of November 29, 2013 — 98
Table 10: Number and Median Size of U.S. Bank Holding Companies and Bank SIFIs as of Third Quarter 2010, Second Quarter 2012, and Second Quarter 2013 (Assets in Billions of Constant 2013 Q2 Dollars) — 106
Table 11: 2013 Large Bank SIFIs' Foreign Legal Entities, as of June 30, 2010, June 30, 2012, and June 30, 2013 — 110

Table 12: Estimated Changes in U.S. Bank SIFIs' Funding Costs and
 Measures of Safety and Soundness Associated with the
 Dodd-Frank Act, from Third Quarter 2010 through Second
 Quarter 2013 122
Table 13: Estimated Changes in Bank SIFIs' Capital Adequacy
 Indicators Associated with the Dodd-Frank Act, from
 Third Quarter 2010 through Second Quarter 2013 124
Table 14: Estimated Changes in Bank SIFIs' Funding Cost and
 Safety and Soundness Indicators Associated with the
 Dodd-Frank Act, from Third Quarter 2010 through Second
 Quarter 2013 125
Table 15: Select Dodd-Frank Rules Implementing Central Clearing
 Swap Reforms Final as of November 15, 2013 126
Table 16: Select Dodd-Frank Rules Implementing Capital and
 Margin Swap Reforms Proposed as of November 15, 2013 127

Figures

Figure 1: Overview of Clearing, Trading, and Reporting
 Requirements under Dodd-Frank Swaps Reforms 44
Figure 2: Trends in Central Clearing of Interest Rate Swaps (by
 Percentage of Gross Notional Value of Swaps), from
 January 2013 through August 2013 49
Figure 3: Percentage of Credit Default Swaps Centrally Cleared (by
 Gross Notional Value of Swaps), from January 2013
 through August 2013 50
Figure 4: Fair Value of Collateral as a Percentage of Net Current
 Credit Exposure from OTC Derivatives Contracts for All
 Counterparty Types Combined, from Second Quarter 2009
 through Second Quarter 2013 52
Figure 5: Fair Value of Collateral as a Percentage of Net Current
 Credit Exposure from OTC Derivatives Contracts by
 Counterparty Type, from Second Quarter 2009 through
 Second Quarter 2013 53
Figure 6: 2013 U.S. Bank SIFIs' Total Assets, as of Second Quarter
 2013 105
Figure 7: Median Market Share for U.S. Bank Holding Companies
 by Size, from First Quarter 2006 through Second Quarter
 2013 107
Figure 8: 2013 U.S. Bank SIFIs' Total Legal Entities, as of June 30,
 2010, June 30, 2012, and June 30, 2013 109

Figure 9: Median Tangible Common Equity as a Percentage of Total
    Assets for Bank Holding Companies by Size, from First
    Quarter 2006 through Second Quarter 2013   112
Figure 10: Median Tangible Common Equity as a Percentage of
    Risk-Weighted Assets for Bank Holding Companies by
    Size, from First Quarter 2006 through Second Quarter
    2013   113
Figure 11: Median Short-Term Liabilities as a Percentage of Total
    Liabilities for U.S. Bank Holding Companies by Size, from
    First Quarter 2006 through Second Quarter 2013   115
Figure 12: Median Liquid Assets as a Percentage of Short-term
    Liabilities for U.S. Bank Holding Companies by Size, from
    First Quarter 2006 through Second Quarter 2013   116

Abbreviations

CDS	credit default swaps
CFPB	Consumer Financial Protection Bureau
CFTC	Commodity Futures Trading Commission
CRA	Congressional Review Act
CSBS	Conference of State Bank Supervisors
Dodd-Frank Act	Dodd-Frank Wall Street Reform and Consumer Protection Act
EGRPRA	Economic Growth and Regulatory Paperwork Reduction Act of 1996
E.O.	Executive Order
FDIC	Federal Deposit Insurance Corporation
Federal Reserve	Board of Governors of the Federal Reserve System
FSOC	Financial Stability Oversight Council
MOU	memorandum of understanding
NCUA	National Credit Union Administration
OCC	Office of the Comptroller of the Currency
OMB	Office of Management and Budget
OTC	over-the-counter
PRA	Paperwork Reduction Act
RFA	Regulatory Flexibility Act
SEC	Securities and Exchange Commission
SIFI	systemically important financial institutions
Treasury	U.S. Department of the Treasury

December 11, 2013

Congressional Addressees

The Dodd-Frank Wall Street Reform and Consumer Protection Act (Dodd-Frank Act) of 2010 requires federal agencies to issue hundreds of regulations to implement the act's requirements.[1] The act responds to the 2007-2009 financial crisis that disrupted the U.S. financial system and threatened not only the solvency of some large financial institutions but also the health of the U.S. economy. Although the financial services industry, academics, and others generally have supported the Dodd-Frank Act's goal of enhancing the stability of the U.S. financial system, the act's provisions and their implementation have been subject to debate. For example, no consensus exists on the extent to which the act will help reduce the likelihood and severity of future financial crises or on the magnitude of the costs that the act and its regulations—individually and cumulatively—will impose on U.S. financial institutions and the economy.[2] Additionally, some market observers have raised concerns about the pace of reform, with some suggesting that reform is occurring too slowly and others arguing that it is moving too quickly.

Federal rulemaking is subject to multiple statutory requirements and executive orders. However, the extent to which the federal financial regulators and other federal agencies are subject to these requirements varies.[3] For example, the Paperwork Reduction Act (PRA) and the Regulatory Flexibility Act (RFA) impose regulatory analysis requirements

---

[1]Pub. L. No. 111-203, 124 Stat. 1376 (2010). We identified 236 provisions of the Dodd-Frank Act that require regulators to issue rulemakings across nine key areas. See GAO, *Financial Regulatory Reform: Regulators Have Faced Challenges Finalizing Key Reforms and Unaddressed Areas Pose Potential Risks*, GAO-13-195 (Washington, D.C.: Jan. 23, 2013).

[2]For example, see GAO, *Financial Regulatory Reform: Financial Crisis Losses and Potential Impact of the Dodd-Frank Act*, GAO-13-180 (Washington, D.C.: Jan. 16, 2013).

[3]We use the term "federal financial regulators" to refer to the Consumer Financial Protection Bureau, Commodity Futures Trading Commission, Federal Deposit Insurance Corporation, Board of Governors of the Federal Reserve System, Office of the Comptroller of the Currency, National Credit Union Administration, and Securities and Exchange Commission.

on federal agencies, including the federal financial regulators.[4] PRA requires agencies to justify collection of information from the public to minimize the paperwork burden and estimate the time and expense needed to comply with the paperwork requirements contained in their rules. RFA requires agencies to assess the impact of their regulation on small entities and consider regulatory alternatives to lessen the regulatory burden on small entities. Under the Congressional Review Act (CRA), before rules can take effect, federal agencies, including the federal financial regulators, must submit their rules to Congress and the Comptroller General, and rules deemed major by the Office of Management and Budget (OMB) generally may not become effective until 60 days after the rules are submitted.[5] For agencies subject to Executive Order 12,866 (E.O. 12,866), such major rules would be considered significant regulatory actions and as such would be subject to formal benefit-cost analysis.[6] However, as independent regulatory agencies, the federal financial regulators are not required to comply with executive orders.[7]

---

[4]Paperwork Reduction Act of 1995, Pub. L. No. 104-13, 109 Stat. 163 (1995) (codified as amended at 44 U.S.C. §§ 3501-3520); Regulatory Flexibility Act, Pub. L. No. 96-354, 94 Stat. 1164 (1980) (codified as amended at 5 U.S.C. §§ 601-612).

[5]Pub. L. No. 104-121, Tit. II, § 251, 110 Stat. 868 (1996) (codified at 5 U.S.C. §§ 801-808). As defined by CRA, a major rule is a rule that OMB finds has resulted in or is likely to result in (1) an annual effect on the economy of $100 million or more; (2) a major increase in costs or prices; or (3) significant adverse effects on competition, employment, investment, productivity, innovation, or on the ability of U.S.-based enterprises to compete with foreign-based enterprises in domestic and export markets. 5 U.S.C. § 804(2). CRA requires agencies to submit to both houses of Congress and the Comptroller General, before rules can become effective, a report containing (i) a copy of the rule, (ii) a concise general statement relating to the rule, including whether it is a major rule, and (iii) the proposed effective date of the rule. 5 U.S.C. § 801(a)(1)(A). Rules not classified as major take effect as otherwise provided by law after submission to Congress, while rules classified as major take effect on the later of 60 days after Congress receives the rule report, or 60 days after the rule is published in the *Federal Register*, as long as Congress does not pass a joint resolution of disapproval. 5 U.S.C. § 801(a)(3), (4). CRA also mandates that we provide a report to Congress that includes an assessment of an agency's compliance with the CRA process. We do not analyze or comment on the substance or quality of rulemaking. We must report to each house of Congress by the end of 15 calendar days after a rule's submission or publication date. 5 U.S.C. § 801(a)(2)(A).

[6]Exec. Order No. 12,866, 58 Fed. Reg. 51,735 (Sept. 30, 1993).

[7]Independent regulatory agencies are those defined by 44 U.S.C. § 3502(5). This statutory definition was revised by the Dodd-Frank Act to include the Office of the Comptroller of the Currency, the Bureau of Consumer Financial Protection, and the Office of Financial Research.

Section 1573(a) of the Department of Defense and Full-Year Continuing Appropriations Act of 2011 amends the Dodd-Frank Act and mandates that GAO conduct an annual study of financial services regulations, including those of the Consumer Financial Protection Bureau (CFPB).[8] We issued our first two reports under this mandate in November 2011 and December 2012.[9] This report examines the

- regulatory analyses conducted by federal agencies in their Dodd-Frank rulemakings, including their assessments of which rules they considered to be major rules;
- interagency coordination by federal agencies in their Dodd-Frank rulemakings and by CFPB with other agencies in its supervision activities; and
- possible impact of selected Dodd-Frank provisions and their implementing regulations and agency plans to assess such regulations retrospectively.

To examine agencies' regulatory analyses and coordination, we focused on final Dodd-Frank rules that became effective from July 24, 2012, through July 22, 2013, a total of 70 rules. To identify these rules, we used a website maintained by the Federal Reserve Bank of St. Louis that tracks Dodd-Frank regulations. We corroborated the data with the federal agencies and data from their websites.

In examining the regulatory analyses of the federal agencies in our review, we reviewed federal statutes, GAO studies, *Federal Register* releases, and other material to identify and summarize the regulatory analyses federal agencies are required to conduct, and conducted, for

---

[8]Pub. L. No. 112-10, § 1573(a), 125 Stat. 38, 138-39 (2011) (codified at 12 U.S.C. § 5496b). We are directed to analyze (1) the impact of regulation on the financial marketplace, including the effects on the safety and soundness of regulated entities, cost and availability of credit, savings realized by consumers, reductions in consumer paperwork burden, changes in personal and small business bankruptcy filings, and costs of compliance with rules, including whether relevant federal agencies are applying sound cost-benefit analysis in promulgating rules; (2) efforts to avoid duplicative or conflicting rulemakings, information requests, and examinations; and (3) other matters deemed appropriate by the Comptroller General. The focus of our reviews is on the financial regulations promulgated pursuant to the Dodd-Frank Act.

[9]GAO, *Dodd-Frank Act Regulations: Implementation Could Benefit from Additional Analyses and Coordination*, GAO-12-151 (Washington, D.C.: Nov. 10, 2011), and *Dodd-Frank Act Regulations: Agencies' Efforts to Analyze and Coordinate Their Rules*, GAO-13-101 (Washington, D.C.: Dec. 18, 2012).

Dodd-Frank rulemakings. Of the 70 rules within our scope, 59 rules were substantive regulations— generally subject to public notice and comment under the Administrative Procedure Act—and required the agencies to conduct some form of regulatory analysis. Of the 59 rules, 10 were classified as major under CRA. For those 10 rules, we compared the regulatory analyses against principles in OMB Circular A-4, which provides guidance on the development of such analyses.[10] To examine how OMB, in consultation with federal agencies, classifies rules as major, we reviewed CRA, agency analyses, *Federal Register* releases of Dodd-Frank major rules, GAO reports, and other materials, and interviewed officials from OMB and federal financial regulators. We relied on our Federal Rules database to identify all Dodd-Frank rules classified as major as of July 22, 2013—36 in total (including the 10 from the specified time period mentioned above).[11]

To examine interagency coordination among the regulators, we reviewed the Dodd-Frank Act, *Federal Register* releases, and GAO reports to identify the interagency coordination or consultation requirements for the 70 rules in our scope. We found evidence of coordination between the rulemaking agency and other regulators for 49 of the 70 rules. We reviewed the *Federal Register* releases of the final rules and interviewed agency officials to document whether the agencies coordinated with other U.S., foreign, or international regulators, either as required by Dodd-Frank or on a voluntary basis. To examine steps CFPB took to comply with Dodd-Frank requirements for interagency coordination and information sharing in its supervision activities, we reviewed the act, CFPB documents, and GAO reports. We also interviewed officials from CFPB and the prudential regulators about such coordination.

Finally, we took a multipronged approach to analyze what is known about the impact of the Dodd-Frank Act on the financial marketplace. First, we

---

[10]As independent regulatory agencies that are not required to follow the economic analysis requirements of E.O. 12,866, the financial regulators also are not required to follow OMB Circular A-4. However, Circular A-4 is an example of best practices for agencies to follow when conducting regulatory analyses, and the financial regulators have told us that they follow the guidance in spirit.

[11]To compile information on all the rules submitted under CRA, we established a database and created a standardized submission form to allow more consistent information collection. Our Federal Rules database is publicly available at www.gao.gov under Legal Decisions & Bid Protests.

updated our indicators monitoring changes in certain characteristics of systemically important financial institutions (SIFI) that might be affected by Dodd-Frank regulations.[12] Second, we updated our economic analysis estimating changes in the (1) cost of credit provided by bank SIFIs and (2) safety and soundness of bank SIFIs. Third, we developed indicators to monitor the extent to which certain of the Dodd-Frank's swap reforms are consistent with the act's goals.[13] As new data become available, we expect to update and, as warranted, revise our indicators and create additional indicators. Fourth, to assess agency plans to conduct retrospective reviews of existing rules, we reviewed executive orders; OMB guidance; *Federal Register* releases, policies, and other agency documents; and GAO reports. Finally, we interviewed agency officials about their plans to conduct retrospective reviews of their Dodd-Frank rules. For parts of our methodology involving the analysis of computer-processed data, we assessed the reliability of these data and determined they were sufficiently reliable for our purposes. (See app. I for a detailed discussion of our objectives, scope, and methodology.)

We conducted this performance audit from January 2013 to December 2013 in accordance with generally accepted government auditing standards. Those standards require that we plan and perform the audit to obtain sufficient, appropriate evidence to provide a reasonable basis for our findings and conclusions based on our audit objectives. We believe that the evidence obtained provides a reasonable basis for our findings and conclusions based on our audit objectives.

---

[12]The Dodd-Frank Act does not use the term "systemically important financial institution" (SIFI). This term is commonly used by academics and other experts to refer to bank holding companies with $50 billion or more in total consolidated assets and nonbank financial companies designated by the Financial Stability Oversight Council for Federal Reserve supervision and enhanced prudential standards under the Dodd-Frank Act. For purposes of this report, we refer to these bank and nonbank financial companies as bank systemically important financial institutions (bank SIFI) and nonbank systemically important financial institutions (nonbank SIFI), respectively. We also refer to nonbank SIFIs and bank SIFIs collectively as SIFIs when appropriate.

[13]A swap is a type of derivative that involves an ongoing exchange of one or more assets, liabilities, or payments for a specified period. Financial and nonfinancial firms use swaps and other over-the-counter derivatives to hedge risk, or speculate, or for other purposes. Swaps include interest rate swaps, commodity-based swaps, and broad-based credit default swaps. Security-based swaps include single-name and narrow-based credit default swaps and equity-based swaps. For the purposes of this report, we use "swaps" to refer to both "swaps" and "security-based swaps."

Background

Financial Services Regulation

The U.S. financial regulatory structure is a complex system of multiple federal and state regulators as well as self-regulatory organizations that operates largely along functional lines. That is, financial products or activities generally are regulated according to their function, no matter which entity offers the product or participates in the activity. The functional regulator approach is intended to provide consistency in regulation, focus regulatory restrictions on the relevant functional areas, and avoid the potential need for regulatory agencies to develop expertise in all aspects of financial regulation.

Prudential Regulators

In the banking industry, the specific regulatory configuration generally depends on the type of charter the banking institution chooses. Depository institution charter types include

- commercial banks, which originally focused on the banking needs of businesses but over time have broadened their services;
- thrifts, which include savings banks, savings associations, and savings and loans and were originally created to serve the needs—particularly the mortgage needs—of those not served by commercial banks; and
- credit unions, which are member-owned cooperatives run by member-elected boards with an historical emphasis on serving people of modest means.

Charters may be obtained at the state or federal level. State regulators charter institutions and participate in the institutions' oversight, but all institutions that have federal deposit insurance have a federal prudential regulator. The federal prudential regulators—which generally may issue regulations and take enforcement actions against industry participants within their jurisdiction—are identified in table 1. Additionally, the Federal Deposit Insurance Corporation (FDIC) insures deposits in banks and thrifts, while the National Credit Union Administration (NCUA) insures deposits in federal and most state-chartered credit unions.

Table 1: Prudential Regulators and Their Basic Functions

Agency	Basic function
Office of the Comptroller of the Currency	Charters and supervises national banks and federal thrifts.
Board of Governors of the Federal Reserve System	Supervises state-chartered banks that opt to be members of the Federal Reserve System, bank holding companies, thrift holding companies and the nondepository institution subsidiaries of those institutions, and nonbank financial companies designated as systemically important financial institutions by the Financial Stability Oversight Council.
Federal Deposit Insurance Corporation	Supervises FDIC-insured state-chartered banks that are not members of the Federal Reserve System, as well as federally insured state savings banks and thrifts; insures the deposits of all banks and thrifts that are approved for federal deposit insurance; and resolves all failed insured banks and thrifts and has been given the authority to resolve large bank holding companies and nonbank financial companies that are subject to supervision by the Board of Governors of the Federal Reserve System and subject to enhanced prudential standards.
National Credit Union Administration	Charters and supervises federally chartered credit unions and insures savings in federal and most state-chartered credit unions.

Source: GAO.

Holding companies that own or control a bank or thrift are subject to supervision by the Board of Governors of the Federal Reserve System (Federal Reserve). The Bank Holding Company Act of 1956 and the Home Owners' Loan Act set forth the regulatory frameworks for bank holding companies and savings and loan holding companies, respectively.[14] The Dodd-Frank Act made the Federal Reserve the regulator of savings and loan holding companies and amended the Home Owners' Loan Act and the Bank Holding Company Act to create certain similar requirements for both bank holding companies and savings and loan holding companies.[15]

Securities and Futures Regulators

The securities and futures markets are regulated under a combination of self-regulation (subject to oversight by the appropriate federal regulator)

---

[14]Bank Holding Company Act of 1956, Pub. L. No. 84-511, 70 Stat. 133 (1956) (codified as amended at 12 U.S.C. §§ 1841-1852); Home Owners' Loan Act, Pub. L. No. 73-43, 48 Stat. 128 (1933) (codified as amended at 12 U.S.C. §§ 1461-1470). Bank holding companies are companies that own or control a bank, as defined in the Bank Holding Company Act. 12 U.S.C. § 1841(a)(1), (c). Savings and loan holding companies are companies that directly or indirectly control a savings association. 12 U.S.C. § 1467a(a)(1)(D).

[15]For a more detailed discussion of the regulatory framework for bank holding companies and savings and loan holding companies, see GAO, *Bank Holding Company Act: Characteristics and Regulation of Exempt Institutions and the Implications of Removing the Exemptions*, GAO-12-160 (Washington, D.C.: Jan. 19, 2012).

and direct oversight by the Securities and Exchange Commission (SEC) and Commodity Futures Trading Commission (CFTC), respectively.[16] SEC regulates the securities markets, including participants such as securities exchanges, broker-dealers, investment companies, and investment advisers. SEC's mission is to protect investors; maintain fair, orderly, and efficient markets; and facilitate capital formation. SEC also oversees self-regulatory organizations—including securities exchanges, clearing agencies, and the Financial Industry Regulatory Authority—that have responsibility for overseeing securities markets and their members; establishing the standards under which their members conduct business; monitoring business conduct; and bringing disciplinary actions against members for violating applicable federal statutes, SEC's rules, and their own rules.

CFTC is the primary regulator of futures markets, including futures exchanges and intermediaries, such as futures commission merchants.[17] CFTC's mission is to protect market users and the public from fraud, manipulation, abusive practices, and systemic risk related to derivatives subject to the Commodity Exchange Act, and to foster open, competitive, and financially sound futures markets. Like SEC, CFTC oversees the registration of intermediaries and relies on self-regulatory organizations, including the futures exchanges and the National Futures Association, to establish and enforce rules governing member behavior. In addition, Title VII of the Dodd-Frank Act expands regulatory responsibilities for CFTC and SEC by establishing a new regulatory framework for swaps. The act authorizes CFTC to regulate "swaps" and SEC to regulate "security-based swaps" with the goals of reducing risk, increasing transparency, and promoting market integrity in the financial system.

Consumer Financial Protection Bureau

The Dodd-Frank Act established CFPB as an independent bureau within the Federal Reserve System and provided it with rule-making, enforcement, supervisory, and other powers over many entities that

---

[16]Certain securities activities also are overseen by state government entities.

[17]Futures commission merchants are individuals, associations, partnerships, corporations, and trusts that solicit or accept orders for the purchase or sale of a commodity for future delivery, among other products, on or subject to the rules of any exchange and that accept payment from or extend credit to those whose orders are accepted. 7 U.S.C. § 1a(28). Firms and individuals who trade futures with the public or give advice about futures trading must be registered with the National Futures Association, the industrywide self-regulatory organization for the U.S. futures industry.

provide consumer financial products and services.[18] Certain consumer financial protection functions from seven federal agencies were transferred to CFPB.[19] CFPB has authority to supervise companies in the mortgage, payday lending, and private student lending markets. As such, CFPB is authorized to supervise certain nonbank consumer financial service companies and insured depository institutions and credit unions with over $10 billion in assets and their affiliates for compliance with federal consumer financial protection laws and related purposes. CFPB does not have authority over most insurance activities or most activities conducted by firms regulated by SEC or CFTC.

Financial Stability Oversight Council (FSOC)

The Dodd-Frank Act established FSOC to identify risks to the financial stability of the United States, promote market discipline, and respond to emerging threats to the stability of the U.S. financial system. The Dodd-Frank Act also established the Office of Financial Research within the U.S. Department of the Treasury (Treasury) to serve FSOC and its member agencies by improving the quality, transparency, and accessibility of financial data and information; conducting and sponsoring research related to financial stability; and promoting best practices in risk management.[20] FSOC's membership consists of the Secretary of the Treasury, who chairs the council; the heads of CFPB, CFTC, FDIC, the Federal Reserve, the Federal Housing Finance Agency, NCUA, the Office of the Comptroller of the Currency (OCC), and SEC; the directors of the Office of Financial Research and the Federal Insurance Office; representatives from state-level financial regulators; and an independent member with insurance experience.

Dodd-Frank Regulations

Under the Dodd-Frank Act, federal financial regulatory agencies are directed or have the authority to issue hundreds of regulations to implement the act's provisions. In some cases, the act gives the agencies

---

[18]12 U.S.C. §§ 5481–5603.

[19]These agencies included the Federal Reserve, FDIC, Federal Trade Commission, Department of Housing and Urban Development, NCUA, the Office of the Comptroller of the Currency, and Office of Thrift Supervision.

[20]12 U.S.C. §§ 5321–5333. For additional information on FSOC and the Office of Financial Research see GAO, *Financial Stability: New Council and Research Office Should Strengthen the Accountability and Transparency of Their Decisions*, GAO-12-886 (Washington, D.C.: Sept. 11, 2012).

little or no discretion in deciding how to implement the provisions. For instance, the Dodd-Frank Act made permanent a temporary increase in the FDIC deposit insurance coverage amount ($100,000 to $250,000); therefore, FDIC revised its implementing regulation to conform to the change. However, other rulemaking provisions in the act appear to be discretionary in nature, stating that (1) certain agencies may issue rules to implement particular provisions or that the agencies may issue regulations that they decide are "necessary and appropriate;" or (2) agencies must issue regulations to implement particular provisions but have some level of discretion over the substance of the regulations. As a result, for these rulemaking provisions, the agencies may decide to promulgate rules for some or all of the provisions, and may have broad discretion to decide what these rules will contain and what exemptions, if any, will apply.

Regulatory Analyses in Federal Rulemaking

As mentioned earlier, federal agencies generally must conduct regulatory analysis pursuant to PRA and RFA, among other statutes, as part of their rulemakings.[21] PRA and RFA require federal agencies, including financial regulators, to assess various impacts and costs of their rules. However, the statutes do not require the agencies to conduct formal benefit and cost analyses that require identification and assessment of alternatives.[22]

In addition to these requirements, authorizing or other statutes require certain federal financial regulators to consider specific benefits, costs, and impacts of their rulemakings. However, none of these statutes, like PRA

---

[21]Paperwork Reduction Act of 1995, Pub. L. No. 104-13, 109 Stat. 163 (1995) (codified as amended at 44 U.S.C. §§ 3501-3520); Regulatory Flexibility Act, Pub. L. No. 96-354, 94 Stat. 1164 (1980) (codified as amended at 5 U.S.C. §§ 601-612). PRA requires agencies to justify any collection of information from the public to minimize the paperwork burden the collection imposes and to maximize the practical utility of the information collected. 44 U.S.C. § 3504. RFA requires federal agencies to (1) assess the impact of their regulation on small entities, including businesses, governmental jurisdictions, and certain not-for-profit organizations with characteristics set forth in the act, and (2) consider regulatory alternatives to lessen the regulatory burden on small entities. 5 U.S.C. § 603.

[22]However, RFA requires agencies to discuss alternatives in the course of a final regulatory flexibility analysis. The analysis must include "a description of the steps the agency has taken to minimize the significant economic impact on small entities consistent with the stated objectives of applicable statutes, including a statement of the factual, policy, and legal reasons for selecting the alternative adopted in the final rule and why each one of the other significant alternatives to the rule considered by the agency which affect the impact on small entities was rejected." 5 U.S.C. § 604(a)(6).

and RFA, prescribe formal, comprehensive benefit and cost analyses that require the identification and assessment of alternatives. Specifically,

- CFTC, under section 15(a) of the Commodity Exchange Act, is required to consider the benefits and costs of its action before promulgating a regulation under the Commodity Exchange Act or issuing certain orders. Section 15(a) specifies that the benefits and costs shall be evaluated in light of (1) protection of market participants and the public; (2) efficiency, competitiveness, and financial integrity of futures markets; (3) price discovery; (4) sound risk-management practices; and (5) other public interest considerations.[23]

- Under the Consumer Financial Protection Act (Title X of the Dodd-Frank Act), CFPB must consider the potential benefits and costs of its rules for consumers and entities that offer or provide consumer financial products and services, including potential reductions in consumer access to products or services resulting from the rules.[24] CFPB also must consider the impacts on insured depository institutions and credit unions with $10 billion or less in assets, and the impacts on consumers in rural areas.[25] When CFPB does not certify that a proposed regulation is not expected to have a significant economic impact on a substantial number of small entities, CFPB also must describe in its initial RFA analysis any projected increase in the cost of credit for small entities and any significant alternatives that would minimize such increases for small entities.[26]

- SEC must consider whether a rule will promote efficiency, competition, and capital formation whenever it is engaged in rulemaking and is required to consider or determine whether an action is necessary or appropriate in the public interest.[27] SEC also must consider the impact that any rule promulgated under the Securities Exchange Act would have on competition.[28] This provision states that

---

[23]§ 15(a), 42 Stat. 998 (1922) (codified as amended at 7 U.S.C. § 19(a)).

[24]Pub. L. No. 111-203, Tit. X, § 1022(b)(2) (codified at 12 U.S.C. § 5512(b)(2)).

[25]*Id.*

[26]5 U.S.C. § 603(d).

[27]Pub. L. No. 104-290, § 106(a)-(c), 110 Stat. 3416, 3424 (1996) (codified as amended at 15 U.S.C. §§ 77b(b), 78c(f), 80a-2(c)). Conforming amendments to the Investment Advisers Act of 1940 were made in section 224 of the Gramm Leach Bliley Act. Pub. L. No. 106-102, § 224, 113 Stat. 1338, 1402 (1999) (codified at 15 U.S.C. § 80b-2(c)).

[28]§ 23(a)(2), 48 Stat. 881 (1934) (codified as amended at 15 U.S.C. § 78w(a)(2)).

a rule should not be adopted if it would impose a burden on competition that is not necessary or appropriate to the act's purposes.
- The Electronic Funds Transfer Act, as amended by the Dodd-Frank Act, requires the Federal Reserve to prepare an analysis of the economic impact of regulations issued by the Federal Reserve that considers the costs and benefits to financial institutions, consumers, and other users of electronic fund transfers.[29] The analysis must address the extent to which additional paperwork would be required, the effects upon competition in the provision of electronic banking services among large and small financial institutions, and the availability of such services to different classes of consumers, particularly low-income consumers.

In contrast, E.O. 12,866, supplemented by Executive Order 13,563 (E.O. 13,563), requires covered federal agencies, to the extent permitted by law and where applicable, to (1) assess benefits and costs of available regulatory alternatives and (2) include both quantifiable and qualitative measures of benefits and costs in their analysis, recognizing that some benefits and costs are difficult to quantify.[30] According to OMB, such analysis can enable an agency to learn if the benefits of a rule are likely to justify the costs and discover which of the possible alternatives would yield the greatest net benefit or be the most cost-effective. In 2003, OMB issued Circular A-4 to provide guidance to federal executive agencies on the development of regulatory analysis as required by E.O. 12,866.[31] The guidance defines good regulatory analysis as including a statement of the need for the proposed regulation, an assessment of alternatives, and an evaluation of the benefits and costs of the proposed regulation and the alternatives. It also standardizes the way benefits and costs of federal

---

[29]15 U.S.C. § 1693b(a)(2).

[30]Exec. Order No. 12,866, 58 Fed. Reg. 51,735 (Sept. 30, 1993). For significant rules, the order further requires agencies to prepare a detailed regulatory (or economic) analysis of both the benefits and costs. More recently, E.O. 13,563 supplemented E.O. 12,866, in part by incorporating its principles, structures, and definitions. Exec. Order No. 13,563, 76 Fed. Reg. 3821 (Jan. 18, 2011). E.O. 12,866 contains 12 principles of regulation that direct agencies to perform specific analyses to identify the problem to be addressed, assess its significance, assess both the benefits and costs of the intended regulation, design the regulation in the most cost-effective manner to achieve the regulatory objective, and base decisions on the best reasonably obtained information available.

[31]OMB, Circular A-4: Regulatory Analysis, September 17, 2003. Circular A-4 refined OMB's "best practices" guidance issued in 1996 and 2000. Executive Order 13,579 (E.O. 13,579) encourages independent regulatory agencies to comply with E.O. 13,563. Exec. Order No. 13,579, 76 Fed. Reg. 41,587 (July 14, 2011).

regulatory actions should be measured and reported. Of the federal agencies included in our review, only FSOC and Treasury are subject to E.O. 12,866. As independent regulatory agencies, the federal financial regulators—CFPB, CFTC, FDIC, the Federal Reserve, OCC, NCUA, and SEC—are not subject to E.O. 12,866 and OMB's Circular A-4. Although not subject to E.O. 12,866 and OMB Circular A-4, most of the federal financial regulators told us that they try to follow Circular A-4 in spirit. In our 2011 report, we found that the policies and procedures of these regulators did not fully reflect OMB guidance and recommended that they incorporate the guidance more fully in their rulemaking guidance.[32] Since then, FDIC, OCC, and SEC revised their guidance as we recommended, but the other agencies have not.[33]

Agencies Conducted Required Regulatory Analyses but May Not Be Identifying All Major Rules

In the *Federal Register* releases of the 59 Dodd-Frank rules that we identified and reviewed, the issuing federal agencies stated that they conducted the regulatory analyses required by various federal statutes.[34] As independent regulatory agencies, the federal financial regulators—CFPB, CFTC, FDIC, the Federal Reserve, OCC, NCUA, and SEC—are not subject to executive orders that require comprehensive benefit-cost analysis in accordance with guidance issued by OMB. Under CRA, OMB is responsible for determining which rules are major but relies on agency analyses to help make the determination. However, our analysis showed that OMB and the agencies may not have applied the CRA criteria consistently in determining which rules are major rules.

---

[32]GAO-12-151.

[33]In April 2013, FDIC updated a statement of policy in the development and review of its regulations and policies. In October 2011, OCC updated its guidance for rulemaking procedures. In March 2012, SEC revised its guidance for conducting economic analysis in SEC rulemakings. All the documents incorporate principles for economic benefit-cost analysis set forth in OMB Circular A-4.

[34]In this report, we use the terms "rules", "regulations", or "rulemakings" generally to refer to *Federal Register* notices of agency action pursuant to the Dodd-Frank Act, including regulations, interpretive rules, general statements of policy, guidance, and rules that deal with agency organization, procedure, or practice.

Regulators Conducted Required Regulatory Analyses for Their Dodd-Frank Rulemakings

Of the 70 Dodd-Frank rules within our scope, 59 regulations were substantive—generally subject to public notice and comment under the Administrative Procedure Act—and required some form of regulatory analysis. These rules were issued individually or jointly by CFPB, CFTC, FDIC, the Federal Reserve, NCUA, OCC, SEC, or Treasury. (See app. II for a list of the regulations in our review.) In examining the regulatory analyses the regulators reported that they conducted for these 59 regulations, we found the following.

- **Agencies conducted the required regulatory analyses.** The agencies conducted regulatory analyses pursuant to PRA and RFA for all 59 rules. In addition, agencies conducted required regulatory analyses pursuant to other statutes, such as the Unfunded Mandates Reform Act of 1995, Small Business Regulatory Enforcement Fairness Act of 1996, and Riegle Community Development and Regulatory Improvement Act of 1994. Agencies also stated that they considered the benefits and costs of their rules as required under their authorizing or other statute. Specifically, CFPB issued 15 rules for which it considered the potential benefits and costs for consumers and entities that offer or provide consumer financial products and services. CFTC and SEC individually or jointly issued 27 rules and considered their potential impact, including their benefits and costs, in light of each agency's required public interest considerations. The Federal Reserve issued one rule and it analyzed the rule's economic impact in consideration of the costs and benefits to financial institutions, consumers, and other users of electronic fund transfers.
- **Agencies identified 10 major rules.** Of the 59 rules that were issued and became effective from July 24, 2012, through July 22, 2013, OMB identified 10 as major rules under CRA. Specifically, CFPB issued two major rules; CFTC issued three major rules; SEC issued two major rules; CFTC and SEC jointly issued one major rule; the Federal Reserve issued one major rule; and the Federal Reserve, FDIC, and OCC jointly issued one major rule.
- **In the 10 major rulemakings, agencies generally addressed the key elements in OMB's guidance.** In our analysis of the 10 Dodd-Frank rules identified as major we found that the agencies addressed many of the OMB guidance's key elements. All of the rules identified the problem to be addressed. In all but two of the rule proposals, the agencies identified regulatory alternative approaches that they considered, and the agencies asked for and received public comments on alternatives in all of the rules. Based on public comments and other information, the agencies analyzed the benefits and costs of the rules, including regulatory alternatives. In 5 of the 10 rules, the agencies explicitly identified the baseline against which they

assessed benefits and costs. In the other rules, the agencies implicitly identified the baseline, typically as pre-Dodd-Frank Act. However, as we found in our last review, the agencies quantified certain compliance costs associated with their rules, such as paperwork-related costs, but generally did not quantify other costs.[35] Furthermore, none of the agencies quantified any of the benefits, in part because of stated data limitations. However, all of the agencies discussed the benefits and costs of their rules, including alternatives, in qualitative terms.

OMB Classified a Number of the Dodd-Frank Rules as Major but, along with Federal Financial Regulators, Used Inconsistent Processes in Applying CRA's Criteria

Since the enactment of the Dodd-Frank Act through July 22, 2013, federal financial regulators and Treasury issued 36 Dodd-Frank rules that were classified as major under CRA. CRA, enacted in 1996, provides Congress with the opportunity to review and disapprove new rules issued by federal agencies.[36] To that end, the act establishes procedures by which Congress may disapprove an agency's rule by introducing a joint resolution of disapproval within 60 days of receiving the rule that, if adopted by both houses of Congress and signed by the President, can nullify the agency's rule.[37]

Specifically, CRA requires agencies, including independent agencies, to submit final rules to Congress and the Comptroller General before the rules can become effective. Rules not classified as major go into effect as otherwise provided by law after submission to Congress and the Comptroller General, while rules classified as major take effect on the later of 60 days after Congress receives the rule report, or 60 days after the rule is published in the *Federal Register*, as long as Congress does not pass a joint resolution of disapproval. During the 60 day period, Congress may introduce, if desired, a resolution of disapproval prior to any major rule taking effect. CRA defines a major rule as any rule that the OMB finds has resulted in or is likely to result in (1) an annual effect on the economy of $100 million or more; (2) a major increase in costs or

---

[35]GAO-13-101.

[36]*See* 5 U.S.C. §§ 801-802.

[37]5 U.S.C. §§ 801(b), 802. Since 1996, 43 resolutions have been introduced in the Senate or House of Representatives and two of those resolutions have passed one house of Congress. Only the Department of Labor's rule on ergonomics (65 Fed. Reg. 68,262 (Nov. 14, 2000)) has been disapproved by both houses of Congress and signed by the President. *See* Pub. L. No. 107-5, 115 Stat. 7 (2001).

prices for consumers; individual industries; federal, state, or local government agencies; or geographic regions; or (3) significant adverse effects on competition, employment, investment, productivity, innovation, or on the ability of United States-based enterprises to compete with foreign based enterprises in domestic and export markets. Although OMB determines whether a rule should be classified as major under CRA, OMB officials told us that they rely on agency submissions of rules and analyses to help make the determination.

Federal financial regulators and Treasury jointly or separately issued the 36 rules pursuant to the Dodd-Frank Act that were found to be major rules. CFPB, CFTC, and SEC collectively accounted for 32 (close to 90 percent) of the rules. (See app. III for a list of Dodd-Frank rules classified as major.) Based on our review of the analyses provided by the agencies to OMB, we found that the agencies expect that all 36 rules will or could meet CRA's first major rule criterion—that is, result in an annual effect on the economy of $100 million or more. In addition, and although a rule needs to meet only one of the multiple criteria in the CRA major rule definition to be considered major, agencies expect that 6 of the 36 major rules could cause a major increase in costs or prices and 3 of the rules could have a significant adverse effect on competition or other activities.

The processes used by federal financial regulators and OMB to identify rules as major vary and create the potential for OMB to not identify all major rules. In 1999, OMB issued guidance on implementing CRA that outlined the process for identifying major rules.[38] For rules subject to E.O. 12,866 review, the guidance instructs agencies, when submitting rules, to indicate whether they consider the rules major. For rules not subject to E.O. 12,866 review, agencies are instructed to contact their OMB desk officer, who has responsibility for certain agencies, in accordance with their established practice. Because the federal financial regulators are not subject to E.O. 12,866, they submit rules to OMB per practices established with their OMB desk officers. Another difference is that agencies subject to E.O. 12,866 generally would be required to prepare a

---

[38]OMB, Memorandum 99-13 (Mar. 30, 1999). The memorandum notes that CRA applies to every executive branch "agency" as defined in 5 U.S.C. § 551(1). This definition, from the Administrative Procedure Act, includes the independent regulatory commissions and boards. In some areas, the memorandum provides different guidance for rules subject to E.O. 12,866 and rules not subject to the order. In this report, we generally refer to agencies subject to E.O. 12,866 as executive branch agencies and agencies not subject to the order as independent regulatory agencies.

comprehensive benefit-cost analysis, quantifying benefits and costs where feasible, for significant regulatory actions. OMB desk officers can then use such analysis in determining whether a rule is major under CRA. In contrast, for rules not subject to the order, the agencies would not necessarily be required to conduct such an analysis. As a result, OMB desk officers may have less complete information from which to determine whether a rule is major under CRA.

We found that regulators' established practices vary. For example, some federal financial regulators told us that they submit all of their rules to OMB for review, but three regulators told us that they submit only those rules they consider major based on their analyses. OMB officials told us that their expectation is that independent agencies should send all rules to their desk officers; otherwise, the desk officers cannot determine whether the rules are major as required under CRA. The risk of OMB not identifying a major rule is unknown, but one federal financial regulator we interviewed said that the agency tries to be conservative in its analyses— tending to overestimate rather than underestimate costs, thereby reducing the risk that a rule may not be identified as major. Additionally, OMB commonly relies on the issuing agency's expertise and analyses to classify rules as major.

We also found examples that indicate that federal financial regulators and OMB may not be interpreting CRA's major rule definition or related OMB guidance consistently.

- **Applying CRA criteria to indirect consequences.** Agencies differed in the way they treated indirect costs of their rules when considering whether such rules could have an impact of $100 million dollars or more annually on the economy. In 2012, CFTC and SEC jointly issued a rule to further define certain swap terms, including swap and security-based swap.[39] In its analysis, CFTC noted that the definitions, by themselves, would not have an annual effect on the economy of $100 million but will affect a number of other rules, including rules determined to be major rules. According to CFTC, these other rules could not be made effective without the final definitions rule; as a result, it concluded that the definitions rule would have an annual effect on the economy of more than $100 million. CFTC and SEC also jointly issued a rule to further define certain

---

[39] 77 Fed. Reg. 48,208 (Aug. 13, 2012).

terms including swap dealer and security-based swap dealer.[40] In its analysis, SEC noted that these definitions, by themselves, would not impose substantive requirements on dealers or major participants, but that the rule should be considered major because it would set boundaries that determine whether entities are subject to other rules, including ones determined to be major rules. In contrast, in 2012 FSOC issued a final rule on the process it intends to use for determining whether a nonbank financial company should be supervised by the Federal Reserve and subject to enhanced prudential standards.[41] Treasury officials noted that they believed the rule should not be considered major because the rule did not impose substantive requirements on any entities, but only laid out the process by which they could become subject to other rules and regulations.[42] OMB agreed with Treasury's assessment and determined that the rule was not major.

- **Applying CRA criteria to related and jointly issued rules.** CFPB combined two separate but related rules to estimate total costs in its CRA major rule assessment, but in other cases, agencies issuing separate but related rules have not combined the rules' costs or benefits. In 2013, CFPB issued two separate mortgage servicing rules that amended Regulation X and Regulation Z.[43] In its CRA analysis submitted to OMB, CFPB estimated that Regulations X and Z would have an annual burden of $22 million in paperwork-related costs, and Regulation X would create an additional annual burden of $90 million.

[40]77 Fed. Reg. 30,596 (May 23, 2012).

[41]77 Fed. Reg. 21,637 (Apr. 11, 2012).

[42]Treasury officials further noted that the actual designation of a nonbank financial company is done on a company-by-company basis in which FSOC members analyze whether a particular company could pose a threat to the financial stability of the United States and then vote to determine whether the company shall be subject to Federal Reserve supervision. A proposed or final determination requires the vote of no fewer than two-thirds of voting FSOC members, including an affirmative vote by the FSOC chairperson. FSOC must provide a written notice of the proposed determination to the nonbank financial company, including an explanation of the basis of the proposed determination. The nonbank financial company may request a hearing to contest the proposed determination in accordance with 12 U.S.C. § 5323(e) and 12 C.F.R. § 1310.21(c).

[43]78 Fed. Reg. 10,696 (Feb. 14, 2013); 78 Fed. Reg. 10,902 (Feb. 14, 2013). Regulation X implements the Real Estate Settlement Procedures Act of 1974 and Regulation Z implements the Truth in Lending Act. The CFPB rules, issued concurrently, amended the regulations and implemented provisions of the Dodd-Frank Act regarding mortgage loan servicing.

GAO-14-67 Dodd-Frank Regulations

CFPB noted that combining the rules results in a total cost of around $112 million and, thus, concluded that the final rules, together, were likely to result in an annual effect on the economy of $100 million or more.[44] OMB agreed and identified both rules as major. In contrast, other federal financial regulators have issued related Dodd-Frank rules, but did not combine them in their CRA analysis. Had these separate but related rules been combined, they may have exceeded the $100 million threshold. Additionally, agencies jointly issued four major Dodd-Frank rules and, in each case, provided their analysis of the costs and benefits to OMB individually rather than cumulatively. OMB has not issued any guidance on the issue of whether rules should be considered separately or together for CRA purposes. OMB officials told us that they expect agencies to coordinate their CRA analyses on jointly issued rules but said such coordination may not always occur.

- **Applying OMB guidance for adding benefits and costs.** OMB classified an SEC rule as major that combined benefits and costs to estimate the rule's annual effect, which could be contrary to its related guidance (discussed below). In 2011, SEC issued a final rule implementing various amendments that the Dodd-Frank Act made to the Investment Advisers Act.[45] In its analysis, SEC noted that it is not able to quantify some of the costs associated with the rule, but the costs it was able to estimate totaled about $55.9 million for the first year. SEC further noted that it was unable to quantify the benefits of the new rules but believes they will be substantial and, together with costs, will result in an annual effect on the economy of more than $100 million. In its February 2011 guidance on E.O. 12,866 regarding economically significant regulatory actions (which does not apply to independent regulatory agencies), OMB noted that under the executive order, agencies must submit a regulatory impact analysis for economically significant regulatory actions, defined (1) to have an annual effect on the economy of $100 million or more or (2) to adversely affect in a material way the economy; productivity; competition; jobs; the environment; public health or safety; or state,

---

[44]CFPB officials told us that the two rules had been considered together in the rulemaking process and were issued on the same date, and that CFPB had combined the CRA analysis of the rules as a matter of efficiency. CFPB officials also told us that CFPB would provide OMB with separate CRA estimates for each individual rule in the future.

[45]76 Fed. Reg. 42,950 (July 19, 2011).

local, or tribal governments or communities.[46] The guidance notes that the $100 million threshold includes benefits, costs, or transfers, and is identical to the threshold for determining whether a rule is major under CRA. The guidance highlighted the word "or" to indicate that benefits and costs should not be combined.

Although OMB issued a memorandum in 1999 to instruct agencies on how to implement CRA, the memorandum provided little guidance on how agencies should apply CRA's major rule criteria—particularly its $100 million threshold. However, as illustrated by our examples, the criteria can be applied in different ways. The only related OMB guidance on applying CRA's $100 million threshold was included in the February 2011 guidance that provided answers to frequently asked questions about the regulatory impact analysis required by E.O. 12,866 and OMB Circular A-4, to which independent regulatory agencies are not subject. According to OMB staff, the guidance was not offered to independent agencies as additional guidance to implement CRA. Without specific guidance addressed to agencies that must comply with CRA on how to apply CRA's $100 million threshold, federal financial regulators may continue to inconsistently apply CRA's major rule criteria and thus, inconsistently advise OMB on whether to classify rules as major. To the extent that any major rules are not being classified as such, those rules may become effective before the end of the 60-day congressional review period required under CRA. On the other hand, our third example also shows that some rules may be potentially misclassified as major and may not be made effective for 60 days after their submission to Congress or publication in the *Federal Register* when such a delay is not required.

Regulators Continue to Coordinate on Rulemakings

Federal agencies coordinated on 49 of the 70 Dodd-Frank regulations that we reviewed, as required by the act or voluntarily. The act also requires CFPB to coordinate with federal and state regulators in its supervision of certain banks and nonbanks that offer or provide consumer financial products or services. To date, CFPB has established a framework to coordinate with prudential regulators and is establishing a similar framework to coordinate with state regulators.

---

[46]OMB, *Regulatory Impact Analysis: Frequently Asked Questions (FAQ)*, accessed on Nov. 13, 2013, http://www.whitehouse.gov/omb/inforeg_regpol_agency_review.

Federal Financial Regulators Have Continued to Coordinate on Their Dodd-Frank Rulemakings

Generally, federal financial regulators recognize the importance of interagency coordination during the rulemaking process. Coordination during the rulemaking process occurs when two or more regulators jointly engage in activities for a purpose such as reducing duplication and overlap in regulations. Effective coordination can help regulators minimize or eliminate staff and industry burden, administrative costs, conflicting regulations, unintended consequences, and uncertainty among consumers and markets. As we reported last year, agency staffs told us that most interagency coordination during rulemaking largely was informal and conducted at the staff level.[47] For example, regulators held some formal interagency meetings early on in the Dodd-Frank rulemaking process, but subsequent coordination on specific rulemakings was mostly informal and conducted through e-mail, telephone conversations, and one-on-one conversations between staff, including several interagency meetings and teleconferences.

Recognizing the importance of coordination, the Dodd-Frank Act imposes interagency coordination or consultation requirements and responsibilities on regulators or in connection with certain rules. Dodd-Frank coordination requirements include topic-specific, agency-specific, and rule-specific requirements. For example:

- Under Title VII, SEC and CFTC must coordinate and consult with each other and prudential regulators, to the extent possible, before starting a rulemaking or issuing an order on swaps or swap-related subjects. This requirement's purpose is to assure regulatory consistency and comparability across the rules or orders. Title VII also directs CFTC, SEC, and the prudential regulators to coordinate with foreign regulators, as appropriate, in implementing swap reform regulations.
- Under Title X of the act, CFPB is required to consult with the appropriate prudential regulators or other federal agencies, both before proposing a rule and during the comment process, on consistency with prudential, market, or systemic objectives administered by such agencies.
- Section 165(i) requires certain financial institutions to conduct annual or semi-annual stress tests and directs regulators to issue consistent and comparable regulations implementing the stress test requirement

---

[47]GAO-13-101.

in coordination with the Federal Reserve and Federal Insurance Office.

- Section 201(b) provides that, for the purpose of defining "financial company," no company shall be deemed to be predominantly engaged in activities that the Federal Reserve has determined are financial in nature or incidental to such financial activities, if the consolidated revenues of that company from such activities constitute less than 85 percentage of the total consolidated revenues of that company, as FDIC, in consultation with Treasury, shall establish by regulation.

We found evidence of coordination between the rulemaking agency and other regulators for 49 of the 70 regulations that we reviewed (see app. IV). We found the act required coordination, or it was unclear whether the act required coordination, in 39 of these 49 rulemakings.[48] We reviewed the rulemakings to document evidence of coordination among the agencies and also interviewed agency staff about their coordination efforts for the 39 rules. We found the following:

- Twelve rules issued by CFTC and SEC implemented provisions in Title VII related to swaps and, thus, required coordination with each other and the prudential regulators to the extent possible.[49] For example, CFTC specified that it coordinated with SEC on nine of the swap-related rules issued solely by CFTC, and with the prudential regulators, among others, on five of these nine rules.
- CFPB indicated that it coordinated with prudential or other federal regulators, pursuant to Title X of the act, on 17 of its rulemakings under federal consumer financial laws.[50] CFPB noted that it consulted or offered to consult with the prudential regulators on all 17 rules and

---

[48]In five of its final rules, CFPB noted in the *Federal Register* releases that although it was unclear about the applicability of the Dodd-Frank coordination requirement to the rules, the agency consulted or coordinated with other regulators as the act would require if applicable. When we refer to the 39 rules where coordination was required, we include these 5 CFPB rules.

[49]CFTC and SEC subject to requirements in the Dodd-Frank Act to issue certain rules jointly. For this review period, CFTC issued 18 rules, SEC issued 9 rules, and they jointly issued 2 rules. The agencies were not required to coordinate under Title VII for all of the rules because, for example, the rules were not related to swaps.

[50]CFPB issued 19 rules during this review period, including 2 joint rules with the Federal Reserve. CFPB coordinated on 17 rules; the other 2 rules were a technical amendment and guidance to which CFPB found the coordination requirement did not apply.

the Federal Trade Commission, the Department of Housing and Urban Development, or other agencies on many of its rules.

- For the other 10 rules where coordination was mandated, we found that CFTC, FDIC, the Federal Reserve, OCC, or SEC coordinated in response to rule-specific interagency coordination requirements in the act.

For 10 of the 49 rules, there was no Dodd-Frank requirement to coordinate, but we found evidence that the agencies voluntarily coordinated on the rulemakings. Most federal financial regulatory officials told us that they generally voluntarily engage in interagency coordination when their rules affect another agency or its supervised entities or when another agency has expertise that can inform their rulemakings.[51]

We also found evidence of international coordination on six swap-related rules in our scope.[52] CFTC issued the six rules and noted that it coordinated with international bodies, such as the European Securities Markets Authority, European Central Bank, and regulators in the United Kingdom, Japan, Hong Kong, Singapore, Sweden, and Canada (see app. IV). CFTC and SEC staffs said that while they may coordinate with international bodies on specific rules, they also are active participants in various international bodies, such as those engaged in global derivatives reforms. For example, CFTC and SEC are members of the International Organization of Securities Commissions' Over-the-Counter (OTC) Derivatives Regulation Task Force, Financial Stability Board's OTC Derivatives Working Group, and OTC Derivatives Regulators' Forum. These groups all work, in part, to share information or encourage

---

[51]We did not find evidence of interagency coordination for 21 of the rules we reviewed. The regulatory agencies were not required to coordinate or did not coordinate, as they determined based on their discretion, on these rules. Agency officials said that some rules were technical in nature and no coordination was needed. For example, officials said some rules were adjustments to existing rules to make them compatible with newly issued rules under the Dodd-Frank Act. Additionally, officials said that some rules were internal and, thus, the agency did not coordinate with other agencies. Examples include rules establishing disclosure requirements or improving recordkeeping standards for supervised entities. We did not evaluate the agencies' rationale for not voluntarily coordinating.

[52]Not all rules issued by CFTC or SEC required international coordination under Title VII of the Dodd-Frank Act. Some of the rules were not related to swaps. For other rules, the agency issuing the rule determined that international coordination was not necessary. For example, officials stated or the rules explained that the agencies did not engage in coordination with foreign regulators because their rules were consistent with rules promulgated by foreign regulators, recommendations issued by international entities, or international standards.

communication and promote consistency in OTC derivatives reforms.[53] CFTC and SEC also have developed supervisory cooperation arrangements or memoranda of understanding (MOU) with foreign authorities in major jurisdictions where regulated entities are located.[54] According to CFTC staff, these coordination efforts may inform CFTC's rulemaking.

In our November 2011 report, we recommended that FSOC work with the federal financial regulators to establish formal coordination policies for rulemaking that clarify issues, such as when coordination should occur, the process that will be used to solicit and address comments, and what role FSOC should play in facilitating coordination.[55] While FSOC has a coordination framework, we found at that time that the framework did not provide, nor according to FSOC staff was it intended to provide, any specifics about staff responsibilities or processes to facilitate coordination. To date, FSOC has not implemented this recommendation. According to FSOC staff, the agency has written protocols for coordinating on rules for which coordination is required under the Dodd-Frank Act. For these and other Dodd-Frank rules, FSOC's Deputies Committee, composed of senior representatives of its members, and six functional committees,

---

[53]The International Organization of Securities Commissions' OTC Derivatives Regulation Task Force coordinates securities and futures regulators' efforts in the supervision and oversight of OTC derivatives markets. The Financial Stability Board's OTC Derivatives Working Group monitors global implementation of OTC derivatives reforms agreed upon by the G20 members. The OTC Derivatives Regulators' Forum is comprised of international financial regulators that have direct authority over OTC derivatives markets. This group meets periodically to exchange views and share information on developments related to OTC derivatives markets. GAO will be issuing a report on international regulatory reforms that will discuss U.S. regulators' participation in international swap reform efforts.

[54]According to CFTC staff, CFTC cooperates with foreign regulatory authorities on a routine basis, both informally and through MOUs and other arrangements. For a list of these agreements, see http://www.cftc.gov/international/memorandaofunderstanding/index.htm. CFTC staff told us that as CFTC issues new regulations related to OTC derivatives reform, staff have developed supervisory cooperation arrangements with foreign authorities in major jurisdictions where regulated entities are located. Staff currently are negotiating arrangements with the European Securities and Markets Authority and authorities in the United Kingdom, Germany, Canada, Australia, Singapore, and Japan, and expect to negotiate arrangements with authorities in other jurisdictions. SEC staff said that SEC has signed MOUs with foreign jurisdictions, including European Securities and Markets Authority and authorities in the United Kingdom, Germany, China, and Turkey.

[55]GAO-12-151.

provide a forum in which agencies can coordinate or consult with each other. The Deputies Committee meets every two weeks to discuss FSOC's agenda and coordinate and oversee the work of the six functional committees. However, as we previously reported, a number of industry representatives believe FSOC could play a greater role in coordinating member agencies' rulemaking efforts.[56] We further noted that the FSOC chairperson, in consultation with the other FSOC members, is required to regularly consult with the financial regulatory entities and other appropriate organizations of foreign governments or international organizations on matters relating to systemic risk to the international financial system. At a March 2013 congressional hearing, an FSOC official testified that Congress did not provide FSOC or its chairperson with authority to require its member agencies to coordinate in all cases, nor did the Dodd-Frank Act change the statutory independence of FSOC's member agencies.[57] He noted that FSOC, nevertheless, will continue to seek to identify ways to further enhance collaboration through FSOC's committees and working groups. We continue to maintain that FSOC, working together with member agencies, should develop formal coordination policies, which could lead to improved coordination of rulemakings.

---

[56]GAO-12-151.

[57]*Who Is Too Big to Fail? GAO's Assessment of the Financial Stability Oversight Council and the Office of Financial Research: Hearing before the Subcomm. On Oversight and Investigations of the H. Comm. on Financial Services.* 113th Cong. 4 (2013) (statement of Amias M. Gerety, Deputy Assistant Secretary, Financial Stability Oversight Council, U.S. Department of the Treasury).

CFPB Has a Framework to Coordinate with Prudential Regulators and Is Establishing One with State Regulators

Under the Dodd-Frank Act, CFPB is authorized to supervise insured depository institutions and credit unions with more than $10 billion in assets (large banks) and their affiliates, and nonbank financial service providers (nonbanks).[58] The statutory requirements for CFPB supervision of large banks and nonbanks largely are the same and include (1) examining such entities to assess, among other things, their compliance with federal consumer financial laws, (2) coordinating with other federal and state regulators, and (3) using, where possible, publicly available information and existing reports from federal or state regulators pertaining to supervised entities. CFPB launched its large bank and nonbank supervision programs in July 2011 and January 2012, respectively. CFPB has established a framework to comply with Dodd-Frank's requirements to coordinate supervision with prudential regulators and is establishing a similar framework to comply with the act's coordination requirements with state regulators.

CFPB Has Established a Framework to Coordinate with Prudential Regulators

While CFPB oversees large banks—that is, insured depository institutions and credit unions with more than $10 billion in assets—and their affiliates for compliance with federal consumer financial laws, prudential regulators also oversee the same entities for safety and soundness purposes and compliance with other laws and regulations. CFPB began operating its large bank supervision program in July 2011 and examining banks shortly thereafter. As of March 31, 2013, CFPB supervised 112 large banks and

---

[58]See sections 1024 and 1025 of the act for CFPB's authority to supervise nonbanks and large banks, respectively. Pub. L. No. 111-203, §§ 1024, 1025 (codified at 12 U.S.C. §§ 5514, 5515). Under section 1025 of the Dodd-Frank Act, CFPB has exclusive examination authority and primary enforcement authority with respect to a bank or credit union with total assets of more than $10 billion and its affiliates and service providers for purposes of assessing compliance with federal consumer financial laws and related purposes. 12 U.S.C. § 5515. Section 1026 provides that the prudential regulators will retain supervisory and enforcement authority with respect to other banks for these purposes. 12 U.S.C. § 5516. Section 1024 authorizes CFPB to supervise certain nondepository entities and individuals who offer or provide mortgage-related products or services, payday loans, private student loans, and larger participants of other consumer financial service or product markets as CFPB defines by rule, among others, plus their service providers. 12 U.S.C. § 5514. Under section 1026, CFPB may include its examiners on a sampling basis at the appropriate prudential regulator's examinations of smaller banks to assess compliance with the requirements of federal consumer financial law. 12 U.S.C. § 5516(c)(1). Additionally, under section 1026, CFPB has supervisory authority over a service provider to a substantial number of smaller banks. 12 U.S.C. § 5516(e). Under section 1029, CFPB may not exercise any authority over certain dealers, subject to exception, that are predominantly engaged in the servicing and sale or leasing of motor vehicles. 12 U.S.C. § 5519(a).

37 affiliated banks.[59] OCC is the prudential regulator for 61 of the large banks, and FDIC, the Federal Reserve, and NCUA are the prudential regulators for 26, 21, and 4 of the other large banks, respectively.

The Dodd-Frank Act requires CFPB and prudential regulators to coordinate their supervision of large banks and their affiliates to minimize regulatory burden. Specifically, CFPB and prudential regulators must (1) coordinate the scheduling of examinations of large banks and their affiliates; (2) conduct simultaneous examinations of large banks and their affiliates, unless otherwise requested by the institution; (3) share draft reports of such examinations with each other and provide the other regulator with at least 30 days to comment on the draft report before finalizing it; and (4) take into consideration any concerns raised by the other regulator before issuing the final examination report.[60] Additionally, the act states that CFPB shall, to the fullest extent possible, use existing reports of supervised entities that have been provided to a federal or state regulator and information that has been reported publicly, and coordinate requirements regarding reports to be submitted by supervised entities.[61]

To meet the statutory requirements for coordination, CFPB has developed a framework to coordinate its supervisory activities with the prudential regulators. The framework consists primarily of (1) an MOU between CFPB and the prudential regulators and (2) CFPB's examination

---

[59]In November 2011, CFPB and the prudential regulators issued an interagency statement explaining that the agencies will use bank Call Reports to determine a bank's asset size for determining which regulator supervises the bank for compliance with federal consumer financial laws. The agencies initially will look to June 30, 2011, Call Report data to determine a bank's asset size. Thereafter, CFPB will become a bank's federal consumer protection law regulator once the bank has reported total assets of greater than $10 billion for four consecutive quarters, and, similarly, a bank will not cease to be regulated by CFPB for such purposes unless it has reported total assets of $10 billion or less for four consecutive quarters.

[60]12 U.S.C. § 5515(b)(2), (e)(1).

[61]12 U.S.C. § 5515(b)(2), (3).

tools, which may be used to help ensure the required coordination is conducted, documented, and reviewed.[62]

MOU for Coordinating. In May 2012, CFPB and the prudential regulators entered into an MOU to facilitate their compliance with Dodd-Frank's coordination requirements.[63] The MOU includes sections that define key terms, establish guidelines for simultaneous and coordinated examinations, and set forth agreements and expectations for sharing information. In light of the act's coordination requirements, the MOU

- establishes guidelines for coordinating examinations, in part by having each regulator designate a point of contact for each bank and affiliates, and directing the points of contact to consult with each other on the scheduling of examinations and to reach agreement on a timetable for sharing scheduling information, such as the scope, estimated start date and duration, and estimated staffing of the examination;
- documents that the regulators generally will conduct their examinations of large banks and their bank affiliates in a simultaneous manner and defines the term "simultaneous examination;"[64]
- documents that CFPB and the relevant prudential regulator will provide the receiving agency at least 30 days to comment on a draft report and will consider any comments provided before finalizing the report; and
- documents that CFPB and the prudential regulators will share material supervisory information, including final supervisory letters or actions; final examination reports, including those related to safety and soundness or financial condition; and other material supervisory

---

[62]CFPB also is a member of the Federal Financial Institutions Examination Council, a formal interagency body empowered to prescribe uniform principles, standards, and report forms for the federal examination of financial institutions. As such, CFPB officials told us that CFPB coordinates its examination procedures with those used by the prudential regulators.

[63]CFPB, *Memorandum of Understanding on Supervisory Coordination,* accessed on November 13, 2013, http://www.consumerfinance.gov/f/201206_CFPB_MOU_Supervisory_Coordination.pdf.

[64]Under the MOU, a simultaneous examination generally is one where material portions of the examinations by the prudential regulator and CFPB are conducted during a concurrent time period and may be carried out either on-site or off-site by either regulator. However, the examinations are not required to be carried out jointly.

GAO-14-67 Dodd-Frank Regulations

information that the CFPB and the prudential regulators agree to share.[65]

According to officials from CFPB and prudential regulators, the MOU serves as a roadmap to guide supervisory coordination, but its implementation is a work in progress. Included in the MOU is a provision under which the agencies agree to review the MOU's operation after the first year of its execution and to consider revisions needed to better accomplish the MOU's objectives. Officials told us that the review currently is underway and may become an annual undertaking.

Examination Coordination Tools. CBPB's Supervision and Examination Manual informs examiners about coordination requirements throughout the four phases of CFPB's examination cycle.[66] For the monitoring phase, where examiners maintain reasonably current information about a bank's activities and risks to consumers or markets, the manual instructs examiners to review supervisory and public information about the bank, including prudential and state regulators' examination reports, and to contact the bank's prudential regulator to discuss any new issues raised by the information. For the pre-examination planning phase, where the examiner-in-charge collects information necessary to determine the examination's scope, resource needs, and work plan, the manual directs the examiner-in-charge to review and update the monitoring information and request other relevant information from prudential and state regulators. In this phase, the examiner-in-charge prepares an information request for the supervised entity with a tailored list of information to be provided to examiners at the examination. In preparing this list, the

---

[65]To facilitate information sharing among regulators, section 1022(c)(6) of the act gives CFPB, upon providing reasonable assurances of confidentiality, access to any report of examination or financial condition made by a prudential regulator or other federal agency having jurisdiction over a supervised entity or service provider, and provides that prudential regulators may, in their discretion, furnish to CFPB any other report or other confidential supervisory information on those entities. 12 U.S.C. § 5512(c)(6)(B). The prudential regulators are accorded the same access to CFPB reports and confidential supervisory information. 12 U.S.C. § 5512(c)(6)(C). To this end, CFPB also has signed information-sharing MOUs with each of the prudential regulators that provide the regulators with reasonable assurances that supervisory information will be treated in a confidential manner.

[66]CFPB, *CFPB Supervision and Examination Manual*, version 2, October 2012. The examination cycle for nonbanks is largely similar to that of large banks, except for the monitoring phase. CFPB continuously monitors each large bank and its affiliates under its jurisdiction. In contrast, CFPB does not continuously monitor nonbanks but instead uses a risk-based analysis to determine which nonbank entities to examine.

manual directs examiners to coordinate the request with prudential and state regulators and keep them abreast of monitoring efforts, correspondence with the supervised entity, and schedule planning. For the examination phase, the manual instructs examiners to communicate regularly with the bank's prudential regulator. Lastly, in closing an examination, the manual instructs the examiner-in-charge to share the examination draft report with the prudential regulator, provide it with no less than 30 days for review and comment, and consider any concerns before issuing a final examination report.

CFPB also has created electronic forms that examiners use to facilitate and document their compliance with the coordination requirements. For example, in the monitoring phase, examiners must complete or update a form to document information about CFPB's coordination with the prudential or state regulators, including examination schedules. For the planning stage, CFPB has created an information request form that includes standardized text to inform the supervised entity that it generally need not provide documents to CFPB that it has provided to prudential regulators. According to CFPB officials, examiners also are instructed to provide the prudential regulator a copy of the information request. In closing the examination, CFPB has a form for preparing the examination letter sent to the supervised entity summarizing the examination findings. The form includes a field for carbon copying the letter to the prudential or state regulator.

The electronic storage of examination workpapers in CFPB's Supervision and Examination System facilitates supervisory review for compliance with, among other things, coordination requirements.[67] All examination workpapers and related documentation (including reports and other information collected from prudential regulators) must be maintained in electronic form and uploaded to the system.[68] As such, the system

---

[67]The Supervision and Examination System is an internal CFPB system that is used to document the supervision process. The system facilitates the creation of schedules, capture of examination information, documentation of the examination process, storage of documents, and ability to run monitoring reports.

[68]According to CFPB's manual, during an examination, examiners collect and review information from the supervised entity to reach conclusions about its practices, its compliance management, and its compliance with specific laws and regulations. The records documenting the review are called workpapers. Workpapers should contain sufficient information and supporting documents to explain the basis for the examination conclusions.

includes records of examination schedules, dates on which examination report drafts were sent to prudential regulators, and comments received from the prudential regulators.[69] Examiners-in-charge and, in turn, management, are required to review and sign off on the adequacy of the workpapers. Such reviews provide a mechanism to help ensure that CFPB is complying with its statutory coordination requirements as delineated in the MOU. In addition, CFPB's manual notes that examination workpapers will be reviewed through an internal quality control process.

Although CFPB has developed these tools to help coordinate examinations with prudential regulators, some members of Congress have raised concerns about CFPB's information collection activities or practices and the potential for overlap between CFPB's information collection efforts and other regulators' efforts. We have ongoing work examining these and related issues for several members of Congress.

CFPB Is Establishing a Framework to Coordinate Its Supervisory Activities with State Regulators

State-chartered banks are subject to the supervision of their state banking regulators. Thus, certain large banks and their affiliates may be supervised by CFPB, a prudential regulator, and a state regulator. In addition, CFPB may share supervisory jurisdiction over certain nonbank entities in the mortgage origination and servicing, private education loan, payday loan, consumer reporting, and debt collection markets with state regulators overseeing these markets.[70] CFPB started examining mortgage lenders, brokers, and servicers and payday lenders in the first

---

[69]While prudential regulators do not have access to the Supervision and Examination System, CFPB may share information in the system with other regulators to fulfill its coordination requirements under the act. As mentioned earlier, CFPB and prudential regulators have entered into information-sharing MOUs that provide the regulators with reasonable assurances that supervisory information will be treated in a confidential manner. CFPB staff stated that CFPB shares information with regulators through secure channels, such as online portals or through encrypted email.

[70]CFPB has the authority to supervise certain nonbanks in the residential mortgage, private education lending, and payday lending markets. CFPB also has the authority to supervise nonbank "larger participants" of markets for other consumer financial products or services, as CFPB defines by rule. 12 U.S.C. § 5514(a)(1). In July 2012 and October 2012, CFPB published final rules defining larger participants of a market for consumer reporting and debt collection markets, respectively. 77 Fed. Reg. 42,874 (July 20, 2012); 77 Fed. Reg. 65,775 (Oct. 31, 2012). CFPB issued a final rule defining larger participants in the student loan servicing market on December 3, 2013 (not yet published in the *Federal Register*).

half of 2012. Since that time, it has also begun examining nonbanks in the consumer reporting and debt collection markets.

The Dodd-Frank Act requires CFPB and state regulators to coordinate their supervision of large banks and nonbanks to minimize regulatory burden.[71] The act states that CFPB shall coordinate supervisory activities, including examinations and requirements regarding information requests, with state regulators.[72] As mentioned earlier, the act also states that CFPB shall, to the fullest extent possible, use existing reports of supervised entities that have been provided to federal or state regulators and information that has been reported publicly.[73] In supervising nonbanks, CFPB must consult with state regulators on requirements or systems, including coordinated or combined systems for registration, where appropriate.[74]

CFPB has entered into agreements with state regulators to address coordination requirements for supervising nonbanks and is beginning to implement those agreements. CFPB established an information-sharing MOU with the Conference of State Bank Supervisors (CSBS) and state regulators in January 2011; according to CFPB officials, over 60 state regulators have signed this or similar MOUs with CFPB.[75] The MOUs memorialize agreements on how to handle and protect any information that is shared, minimize burden on supervised entities, and promote consistent examination standards, primarily through the development of a

---

[71]See 12 U.S.C. §§ 5514(b)(3), 5515(b)(2).

[72]See 12 U.S.C. §§ 5514(b)(3), 5515(b)(2), (e)(2).

[73]See 12 U.S.C. §§ 5514(b)(4), 5515(b)(3). As with prudential regulators, to facilitate information sharing among regulators, section 1022(c)(6)(C) of the act gives regulators having jurisdiction over a covered person or service provider, including state regulators, access to any report of examination made by CFPB with respect to that supervised entity or service provider, upon providing reasonable assurances of confidentiality.

[74]See 12 U.S.C. §§ 5512(c)(7)(C), 5514(b)(7)(D).

[75]CSBS is the nationwide organization of banking regulators from all 50 states, the District of Columbia, Guam, Puerto Rico, and the U.S. Virgin Islands. Besides the MOU, on December 6, 2012, CFPB also issued a Statement of Intent for Sharing Information with state banking and financial services regulators that spells out specific items that CFPB intends to share with state regulators, including examination schedules, examination reports, consumer complaint information, among others.

framework for coordinating supervisory activities.[76] In May 2013, CFPB and CSBS, on behalf of the state regulators, agreed on a supervisory coordination framework. As part of the framework, CFPB and CSBS agreed to establish a State Coordinating Committee that would be in charge of coordinating with CFPB on nonbank supervision.[77] CFPB officials told us that CFPB and state regulators are implementing the framework but much work remains.

CFPB has not yet undertaken rulemakings to require nonbanks to register and, thus, has not formally begun efforts to coordinate registration systems with state regulators. According to its website, the Nationwide Mortgage Licensing System, owned and maintained by the State Regulatory Registry, LLC, a wholly-owned subsidiary of CSBS, is the sole system for licensing mortgage companies for 54 state agencies and the sole system for licensing mortgage loan originators for 58 state and territorial agencies.[78] In February 2012, CSBS stated that it intends to expand the system to other markets and, in April 2012, announced that five state banking agencies were expanding their use of the system to

---

[76]Specifically, in the January 2011 MOU, CFPB and CSBS agreed to consult on the practices used by the state regulators in examining providers of consumer financial products and services. CSBS agreed to provide CFPB with information furnished to it by state regulators and other relevant multistate bodies on examination processes, including examination manuals, standardized information requests, and examination procedures. Additionally, CFPB, CSBS, and state regulators agreed to consult on and jointly develop training programs for examiners.

[77]Under the framework, CFPB, state banking regulators, and the State Coordinating Committee are to establish a point of contact for each supervised entity, share examination schedules annually and review them at least quarterly, and have a joint examiner-in-charge, if appropriate. In addition, points of contact are instructed to develop and update a supervision plan for each supervised entity tailored to the entity's organizational structure and risk profile. Lastly, the framework directs CFPB and the State Coordinating Committee to compile annual lists of all covered nonbank entities and nonbank entities subject to examination.

[78]The Nationwide Mortgage Licensing System is a web-based system that allows state licensed mortgage lenders, mortgage brokers, and loan officers to apply for, amend, update, or renew a license online for all participating state agencies using a single set of uniform applications. Mortgage loan originators are required by the SAFE Mortgage Licensing Act of 2008 to be state licensed or registered through the Nationwide Mortgage Licensing System. Pub. L. No. 110-289, Div. A, Tit. V, § 1504(a), 122 Stat. 2810 (2008) (codified at 12 U.S.C. § 5103(a)).

license and supervise nonbanks beyond the mortgage industry.[79] CFPB officials told us that the agency has not yet determined when it will issue rulemakings on registration of nonbanks. They said they have engaged in discussions with CSBS to determine whether and how CFPB should leverage that system for registering nonbanks but no determinations have been made.

Impacts of the Dodd-Frank Act Are Uncertain, and Regulators Are Developing Plans to Review Rules Retrospectively

Federal financial regulators are continuing to implement reforms pursuant to the Dodd-Frank Act, but the full impact of the act remains uncertain. This uncertainty stems from a number of factors. In particular, the implementation of the reforms is being driven largely by rulemakings or other regulatory actions, but not all rules are finalized and effective. In addition, even when the act's reforms are fully implemented, it will take time for the financial services industry to comply with the array of new regulations—meaning additional time will need to elapse to measure the impact of the rules. Moreover, the evolving nature of implementation makes isolating the Dodd-Frank Act's effect on the U.S. financial marketplace difficult. This task is confounded by the many factors that can affect the financial marketplace, including factors that could have an even greater impact than the act.

Recognizing these limitations and difficulties, we developed a multipronged approach to analyze current data and trends that might be indicative of some of the Dodd-Frank Act's initial impacts, as institutions react to issued and expected rules. First, we updated the indicators that we developed in our December 2012 report to monitor changes in certain characteristics of SIFIs, which are subject to enhanced prudential standards and oversight under the act.[80] Although the indicators may be

---

[79]With the implementation of updated uniform Nationwide Mortgage Licensing System licensing forms, state regulatory agencies in Massachusetts, Oklahoma, Rhode Island, Vermont, and Washington are managing license authorities covering a range of industries, including money transmitters, debt collectors, and sales finance companies.

[80]See GAO-13-101. The Dodd-Frank Act does not use the term "systemically important financial institution" (SIFI). This term is commonly used by academics and other experts to refer to bank holding companies with $50 billion or more in total consolidated assets and nonbank financial companies designated by the Financial Stability Oversight Council for Federal Reserve supervision and enhanced prudential standards under the Dodd-Frank Act. For purposes of this report, we refer to these bank and nonbank financial companies as bank systemically important financial institutions (bank SIFI) and nonbank systemically important financial institutions (nonbank SIFI), respectively. We also refer to nonbank SIFIs and bank SIFIs collectively as SIFIs when appropriate.

suggestive of the act's impact, they do not identify causal links between their changes and the act. Further, many other factors can affect SIFIs and, thus, the indicators. Second, we also updated our difference-in-difference analysis to infer the act's impact on the provision of credit by and the safety and soundness of bank SIFIs. The analysis is subject to limitations, in part because factors other than the act could be affecting these entities. Third, we developed indicators to monitor the extent to which certain of the Dodd-Frank Act's swap reforms are consistent with the act's goals of reducing risk. Like our SIFI indicators, our swap indicators have limitations. For example, they do not identify causal links between changes in swap markets and the act or its regulations. Finally, we assessed agencies' plans to conduct retrospective reviews of their existing rules.

Indicators Suggest Increased Resilience and Size of Large SIFIs between the Third Quarter of 2010 and the Second Quarter of 2013

According to its legislative history, the Dodd-Frank Act contains provisions intended to reduce the risk of failure of a large, complex financial institution and the damage that such a failure could do to the economy.[81] Such provisions include (1) authorizing FSOC to designate a nonbank financial company for Federal Reserve supervision if FSOC determines it could pose a threat to U.S. financial stability and (2) directing the Federal Reserve to impose enhanced prudential standards and oversight on bank holding companies with $50 billion or more in total consolidated assets (referred to as bank SIFIs in this report) and nonbank financial companies designated by FSOC (referred to as nonbank SIFIs in this report). Federal agencies and regulators have been working to implement these provisions. For example, in January and December 2012, the Federal Reserve proposed its enhanced prudential standards rules for certain U.S. and foreign companies operating in the United States, respectively, and has finalized rules implementing some of these standards.[82] In addition, FSOC designated two nonbank financial companies in July 2013 and a third in September 2013. (See app. V for a summary of SIFI-related provisions and their rulemaking status.)

As we reported last year, the Dodd-Frank Act and its implementing rules may result in adjustments to SIFIs' size, interconnectedness, complexity,

---

[81]S. Rep. No. 111-176 (2010).

[82]77 Fed. Reg. 594 (Jan. 5, 2012); 77 Fed. Reg, 76,628 (Dec. 28, 2012). See appendix V for a summary of select finalized SIFI-related rulemakings.

leverage, or liquidity over time.[83] We developed indicators to monitor changes in some of these SIFI characteristics. The size and complexity indicators reflect the potential for a single company's financial distress to affect the financial system and economy. The leverage and liquidity indicators reflect a SIFI's resilience to shocks or its vulnerability to financial distress. Like we did in our last report, we continue to focus our analysis on bank SIFIs, given that FSOC only recently designated three nonbank financial companies for Federal Reserve supervision.[84] Our indicators have limitations. For example, the indicators do not identify causal links between changes in SIFI characteristics and the act. Rather, the indicators track changes in the size, complexity, leverage, and liquidity of SIFIs over the period since the Dodd-Frank Act was passed to examine whether the changes are consistent with the goals of the act. However, other factors—including the economic downturn, international banking standards agreed upon by the Basel Committee on Banking Supervision (Basel Committee), European debt crisis, and monetary policy actions—also affect bank holding companies and, thus, the indicators.[85] These factors may have a greater effect than the Dodd-Frank Act on SIFIs. Furthermore, because a number of rules implementing SIFI-related provisions have not yet been finalized, our indicators include the effects of these rules only insofar as SIFIs have changed their behavior in response to issued rules and in anticipation of expected rules. In this regard, our indicators provide baselines against which to compare future trends.

Table 2 summarizes the changes in our bank SIFI indicators from the third quarter of 2010 through the second quarter of 2013 and allows for

---

[83]See GAO-13-101.

[84]Our analyses of bank SIFIs include U.S. bank holding companies with total consolidated assets of $50 billion or more and foreign bank organizations' U.S.-based bank holding company subsidiaries that on their own have total consolidated assets of $50 billion or more.

[85]The Basel Committee has agreed on a new set of risk-based capital, leverage, liquidity, and other requirements for banking institutions (Basel III requirements). Additionally, the Financial Stability Board and the Basel Committee have agreed on new capital and other requirements applicable to designated globally systemically important banks (G-SIB requirements). U.S. banking regulators have implemented some of these requirements, and the Federal Reserve has indicated its intention to base some of the SIFI enhanced prudential standards on the Basel III and G-SIB requirements. For more details see appendix V.

the following observations. (See app. VI for more details on our indicators.)

- First, the total number of bank SIFIs declined by three, including one large bank SIFI, over the period.[86] Median assets and median market share (measured in assets) for large bank SIFIs increased over the period. Even with one less large bank SIFI by mid-2013, the increase in the size of large bank SIFIs is consistent with an increase in the spillover effect posed by such SIFIs—that is, the potential for such a company's financial distress to affect the financial system and economy. In contrast, median assets and median market share declined for other bank SIFIs over the period; these trends are consistent with a decrease in the spillover effects of those bank SIFIs.
- Second, our complexity indicator suggests that large U.S. bank SIFIs in the second quarter of 2013 continue to be relatively more complex than other U.S. bank SIFIs, but they generally decreased their total number of legal entities over the period. In addition, four 2013 large bank SIFIs decreased their number or percentage of foreign legal entities, while the number of countries where their foreign legal entities operated decreased or remained stable over the period. In contrast, two 2013 large bank SIFIs increased both their number and percentage of foreign legal entities, and for one of them the number of countries where its foreign entities operated increased by 50 percent. Because of the mixed trends, the change in the spillover effects is unclear.
- Third, our indicators suggest that bank SIFIs, on average, have decreased their leverage from the third quarter of 2010 to the second quarter of 2013, although one of our measures shows that leverage for bank SIFIs did not change substantially from mid-2012 to mid-2013. Similarly, our liquidity indicators show that bank SIFIs improved their liquidity over the period, although one of our measures shows that large bank SIFIs' liquidity deteriorated from mid-2012 to mid-2013. Despite these recent trends, the changes in our leverage and liquidity indicators from the third quarter of 2010 through the second quarter of 2013 are consistent with an improvement in SIFIs' resilience to shocks or vulnerability to financial distress.

---

[86]In our November 2012 report, we noted that there were seven large bank SIFIs as of the second quarter of 2012. Six of them continue to be large bank SIFIs as of the third quarter of 2013. In February 2013, the remaining one received regulatory approval to deregister as a bank holding company.

Table 2: Summary of Trends in Indicators for Bank SIFIs, from Third Quarter 2010 through Second Quarter 2013

Characteristic	Indicator (italicized) and description of trend	Consistent with decreased, no change, or increased spillover effects or resilience?
Size – Size captures the amount of financial services or financial intermediation that a bank holding company provides.	The *number of large bank SIFIs* declined by one, and the *number of other bank SIFIs* declined by two. Median *assets for large bank SIFIs* increased and median assets for *other bank SIFIs* decreased. The median *market share (measured in assets) for large bank SIFIs* increased and median *market share for the other bank SIFIs* decreased.	Consistent with an increase in spillover effects of large bank SIFIs. Consistent with a decrease in spillover effects of other bank SIFIs.
Interconnectedness – Interconnectedness captures direct or indirect linkages between financial institutions that may transmit distress from one institution to another.	None	N/A
Complexity – Operational complexity may reflect an institution's diverse lines of business and locations in which the institution operates.	The *median number of legal entities for large bank SIFIs* decreased from 4,991 to 3,682.[a] Four large bank SIFIs decreased their *number or percentage of legal entities located outside of the United States*, and the *number of countries where their foreign entities* are located remained stable or decreased. For the two other large bank SIFIs, the *number and percentage of foreign legal entities* increased and, for one of them, the *number of countries where the foreign entities are located* increased.	Unclear
Leverage – Leverage can be defined broadly as the ratio between some measure of risk exposure and capital that can be used to absorb unexpected losses from the exposure. Traditionally, it has referred to the use of debt, instead of equity, to fund an asset and been measured by the ratio of total assets to equity on the balance sheet.	The median *tangible common equity as a percentage of total assets for large and other bank SIFIs* increased. The median *tangible common equity as a percentage of risk-weighted assets for large and other bank SIFIs* increased.	Consistent with an increase in resilience
Liquidity – Liquidity represents the ability of an institution to fund its assets and meet its obligations as they become due.	The median *short-term liabilities as a percentage of total liabilities for large and other bank SIFIs* decreased. The median *liquid assets as a percentage of short-term liabilities for large and other bank SIFIs* increased.	Consistent with an increase in resilience

Sources: GAO analysis of data from the Federal Reserve Bank of Chicago, Bureau of Economic Analysis, and Federal Reserve Board.

[a]Trends for our complexity indicators descr be changes from June 30, 2010, through June 30, 2013.

Note: Large bank SIFIs are those with $500 billion or more in assets. Other bank SIFIs are those with assets between $50 billion and $500 billion. To calculate the median measures, we calculated the relevant indicator measure for each bank holding company, and then reported the median for large bank SIFIs, the median for other bank SIFIs, the median for non-SIFI banks, or the median for the entire group. See appendix VI for additional information on our SIFI indicators.

Enhanced Prudential Standards Are Associated with Improved Safety and Soundness of Bank SIFIs but Not with Changes in the Cost of Credit since Mid-2010

According to our updated regression analysis, the Dodd-Frank Act has not been associated with a change in the cost of credit provided by U.S. bank SIFIs, but has been associated with an increase in the safety and soundness of the SIFIs.[87] As we have noted, the Dodd-Frank Act requires the Federal Reserve to impose a variety of regulatory reforms on SIFIs, including enhanced risk-based capital, leverage, and liquidity requirements. These reforms may affect the safety and soundness of bank SIFIs and the cost and availability of credit provided by bank SIFIs. Although capital and leverage requirements may help reduce the probability of bank failures and promote financial stability, they could cause banks to raise lending rates and limit their ability to provide credit, especially during a crisis. Similarly, while stricter liquidity requirements may help reduce the probability of bank failures and promote financial stability, banks could respond to these requirements by increasing lending spreads to offset lower yields on assets or longer maturities on liabilities. To the extent that they increase the cost and reduce the availability of credit, these reforms may lead to reduced output and economic growth.[88]

Our econometric analysis assesses the initial impact of the Dodd-Frank Act's new requirements for bank SIFIs on (1) the cost of credit they provide and (2) their safety and soundness. Our analysis leverages the Dodd-Frank Act's requirement that bank holding companies with total consolidated assets of $50 billion or more are subject to enhanced regulation by the Federal Reserve but other bank holding companies are not. Specifically, we compare funding costs, capital adequacy, asset quality, earnings, and liquidity for bank SIFIs and non-SIFI bank holding companies before and after the enactment of the Dodd-Frank enhanced

---

[87]See appendix VII for more information on our econometric analysis.

[88]See, for example, Basel Committee on Banking Supervision, *An Assessment of the Long Term Economic Impact of Stronger Capital and Liquidity Requirements* (Basel, Switzerland, August 2010), and Basel Committee on Banking Supervision and Financial Stability Board, *Assessing the Macroeconomic Impact of the Transition to Stronger Capital and Liquidity Requirements* (Basel, Switzerland, August 2010).

prudential requirements. All else being equal, the difference in the comparative differences is the inferred effect of the Dodd-Frank Act's prudential requirements on bank SIFIs.

Our approach allows us to partially differentiate changes in funding costs, capital adequacy, asset quality, earnings, and liquidity associated with the Dodd-Frank Act from changes due to other factors. However, several factors make isolating and measuring the impact of the Dodd-Frank Act's new requirements for SIFIs challenging. The effects of the act cannot be differentiated from the effects of simultaneous changes in economic conditions, such as the pace of the recovery from the recent recession, or regulations, such as those stemming from Basel III, or other changes, such as in credit ratings that differentially may affect bank SIFIs and other bank holding companies. In addition, many of the new requirements for SIFIs have yet to be implemented. For example, the Federal Reserve is required to implement enhanced prudential standards, including capital requirements, stress testing, liquidity requirements, single-counterparty credit limits, an early remediation regime, and risk-management and resolution planning. Only rules for resolution planning and stress testing have been finalized.[89] Additionally, the Federal Reserve has proposed to implement a quantitative liquidity requirement for bank holding companies, savings and loan holding companies, and depository institutions with more than $250 billion in total assets and has indicated that it plans to impose a capital surcharge on the largest SIFIs. Nevertheless, our estimates are suggestive of the initial effects of the Dodd-Frank Act on bank SIFIs and provide a baseline against which to compare future trends.

Our estimates suggest that the Dodd-Frank Act has not been associated with a significant change in U.S. bank SIFIs' funding costs (table 3). To the extent that the cost of credit provided by bank SIFIs is a function of their funding costs, the new requirements for SIFIs likely have had little effect on the cost of credit to date.

---

[89]See appendix V for the rulemaking status of the enhanced prudential standards.

Table 3: Estimated Changes in U.S. Bank SIFIs' Funding Costs and Measures of Safety and Soundness Associated with the Dodd-Frank Act, from Third Quarter 2010 through Second Quarter 2013

Variable	Measured as	Estimated change and standard error of estimated change (percentage points)	Estimated change statistically significant at the five percent level?
Cost of credit indicator			
Funding cost	Interest expense as a percentage of interest-bearing liabilities	0.02 (0.02)	No
Safety and soundness indicators			
Capital adequacy	Tangible common equity as a percentage of total assets	1.50 (0.22)	Yes
	Tangible common equity as a percentage of risk-weighted assets	2.02 (0.36)	Yes
Asset quality	Performing assets as a percentage of total assets	0.41 (0.13)	Yes
Earnings	Earnings as a percentage of total assets	0.09 (0.03)	Yes
Liquidity	Liquid assets as a percentage of volatile liabilities	-1.80 (8.87)	No
	Stable liabilities as a percentage of total liabilities	5.12 (1.01)	Yes

Source: GAO analysis of data from the Federal Reserve Bank of Chicago.

Notes: We analyzed data for top-tier bank holding companies that filed form FR Y-9C from the first quarter of 2006 through the second quarter of 2013. We estimated the effects of the new SIFI requirements on bank SIFIs by regressing the variables listed in the table on indicators for each bank holding company, indicators for each quarter, indicators for whether a bank holding company is a SIFI for quarters from the third in 2010 through the second in 2013, and other variables controlling for size, foreign exposure, securitization income, other nontraditional income, and participation in the Troubled Asset Relief Program. Estimated changes are the coefficients on the indicators for whether a bank holding company is a SIFI in quarters from the third in 2010 through the second in 2013. We used t-tests to assess whether the coefficient on the SIFI indicator was significant at the 5 percent level. For more information on our methodology, see appendix VII.

Our estimates also suggest that the Dodd-Frank Act is associated with improvements in most measures of U.S. bank SIFIs' safety and soundness. As shown in table 3, bank SIFIs appear to be holding more capital than they otherwise would have held in every quarter since the Dodd-Frank Act was enacted. The quality of assets on the balance sheets of bank SIFIs also seems to have improved since the Dodd-Frank Act was enacted. The act is associated with higher earnings for bank SIFIs in the time period after the act's enactment. It is also associated with improved liquidity as measured by the extent to which a bank holding company is using stable sources of funding. The only measure that has not clearly improved since the act's enactment is liquidity as measured by the capacity of a bank holding company's liquid assets to cover its volatile liabilities. Thus, the Dodd-Frank Act appears to be broadly associated with improvements in most indicators of safety and soundness for U.S. bank SIFIs. (See app. VII for more details on our regression analysis.)

Swaps Indicators Provide Baselines for Assessing the Future Impact of Some Swap Reforms

In general, swaps are types of derivative contracts that involve ongoing exchanges of one or more assets, liabilities, or payments for a specified period. For example, swaps can be used to exchange fixed-rate interest payments for floating interest payments based on market rates (one type of interest rate swap), or to protect against the default of a bond issuer (one type of credit default swap). Financial and nonfinancial firms use swaps and other derivatives to hedge risk, to speculate, or for other purposes. Unlike futures, which are standardized financial contracts that are traded on exchanges, swaps traditionally have been privately negotiated between two counterparties in the over-the-counter (OTC) market. Swaps include interest rate swaps, commodity-based swaps, equity swaps, and credit default swaps.

In varying degrees and ways, swaps and other OTC derivatives played a role in the most recent financial crisis. As FSOC reported, credit default swaps (CDS), including AIG's large holdings of such swaps, exacerbated the crisis because they were not well understood by regulators or market participants.[90] FSOC also noted that OTC derivatives generally were a factor in the propagation of risks during the recent crisis because of their complexity and opacity, which contributed to excessive risk taking, a lack of clarity about the ultimate distribution of risks, and a loss in market confidence. In that regard, the crisis illustrated that swaps and other OTC derivatives can contribute to systemic risk in at least two ways. First, while swaps can be used to manage risk and increase liquidity, swaps generally have not been subject to regulatory requirements for margin (i.e., collateral based on the market value of the swap). This allowed some swap participants to take large speculative positions using a relatively small amount of capital, thereby increasing leverage. Second, swaps increased the interconnectedness of the financial system by exposing many banks, financial entities, and end-users to the credit risk of a small number of swap dealers. The concentration of most OTC

---

[90]FSOC, Annual Report, 2011.

derivatives trading among a small number of dealers created the risk that the failure of one of these dealers could expose counterparties to sudden losses and destabilize financial markets.

Title VII of the Dodd-Frank Act establishes a new regulatory framework for swaps. The act authorizes CFTC to regulate "swaps" and SEC to regulate "security-based swaps" with the goals of reducing risk, increasing transparency, and promoting market integrity in the financial system. Title VII includes the following four major swaps reforms.

- **Registration and regulation.** The title provides for the registration and regulation of swap dealers and major swap participants, including subjecting them to (1) prudential regulatory requirements, such as minimum capital and minimum initial and variation margin requirements and (2) business conduct requirements to address, among other things, interaction with counterparties, disclosure, and supervision.[91]
- **Mandatory clearing.** The title imposes mandatory clearing requirements on swaps, but exempts, among others, certain end users that use swaps to hedge or mitigate commercial risk.[92]
- **Exchange trading.** The title requires swaps subject to mandatory clearing to be executed on an organized exchange or swap execution facility, unless no facility offers the swap for trading.[93]
- **Mandatory reporting.** The title requires all swaps to be reported to a registered swap data repository or, if no such repository will accept the swap, to CFTC or SEC, and subjects swaps to post-trade transparency requirements (real-time public reporting of certain swap data).

---

[91]In general, minimum capital requirements are designed to provide firms with sufficient liquidity to meet unsubordinated obligations to customers and counterparties and sufficient resources to wind down in an orderly manner without the need for a formal proceeding. Minimum margin requirements are generally intended to regulate the amount of credit directed into swaps and related transactions and to help protect swaps entities and their customers from price fluctuations and against losses arising from undue leverage. Minimum margin requirements also can help manage counterparty credit risk.

[92]Any entity acting as a clearinghouse, or central counterparty, must register with CFTC, SEC, or both, as appropriate (unless granted an exemption) and is subject to regulatory requirements established by CFTC, SEC, or both, as appropriate.

[93]Organized exchanges and swap execution facilities are subject to comprehensive registration, and operational and self-regulatory requirements.

Figure 1 illustrates these reforms and some of the differences between swaps traded on exchanges and cleared through clearinghouses and swaps traded in the OTC market.

Figure 1: Overview of Clearing, Trading, and Reporting Requirements under Dodd-Frank Swaps Reforms

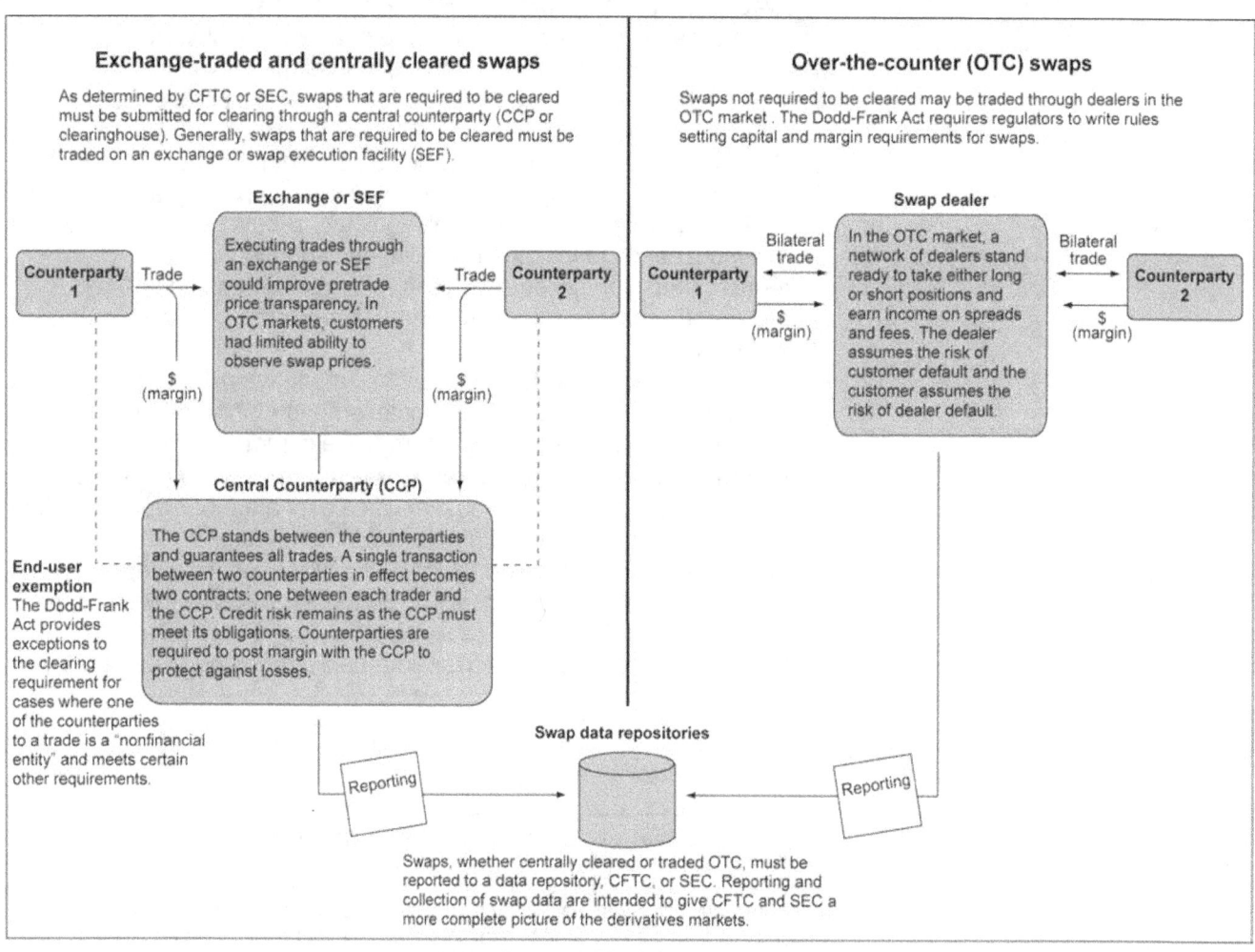

Source: GAO analysis of the Dodd-Frank Act.

According to the Dodd-Frank Act's legislative history, key elements for reducing systemic risk include increasing the use of central clearinghouses and appropriate margining and capital for OTC derivatives.[94] CFTC and SEC have issued final rules to implement many of the regulatory frameworks for clearing standardized swaps. In December 2012, CFTC issued a final rule establishing the first clearing requirement for four types of interest rate swaps and two types of CDSs.[95] In July 2012, SEC issued a final rule on, among other things, the process that the agency will use to determine whether a security-based swap is required to be cleared but has not yet subjected any security-based swaps to the clearing requirement.[96] CFTC, SEC, and the prudential banking regulators have proposed rules to implement Dodd-Frank's margin and capital requirements for swap entities, but as of September 2013, these rules have not yet been finalized.[97] (See app. VIII for tables listing select Dodd-Frank swap reform related rulemakings.)

Once fully implemented, some provisions in Title VII of the act may help achieve the goal of reducing risk, in part by increasing the central clearing of swaps and posting of margin for uncleared swaps. We developed two sets of indicators to measure changes in (1) the central clearing of swaps and (2) the use of margin collateral for OTC derivatives. In this report, these indicators provide a baseline for measuring future changes in the central clearing of swaps and use of margin collateral, as the Dodd-Frank swap reforms have not been fully implemented. In future reports, we plan to update these indicators to determine whether changes in central clearing and the use of margin collateral are consistent with the act's swap reforms. Importantly, these indicators have several key limitations. First, changes in our indicators do not necessarily suggest a change in risk, because the intended outcomes of the swap reforms may not necessarily reduce systemic risk. For instance, experts, including those

---

[94]S. Rep. No. 111-176 (2010).

[95]77 Fed. Reg. 74,284 (Dec. 13, 2012). The types of interest rate swaps subject to mandatory clearing are fixed rate to floating rate swaps, floating rate to floating rate swaps, overnight index swaps, and forward rate agreements. The two types of CDSs subject to mandatory clearing are North American untranched CDS Indices and European untranched CDS Indices.

[96]77 Fed. Reg. 41,602 (July 13, 2012).

[97]See Capital, Margin, and Segregation Requirements for Security-Based Swap Dealers and Major Security-Based Swap Participants and Capital Requirements for Broker-Dealers, 77 Fed. Reg. 70,214 (Nov. 23, 2012); Margin and Capital Requirements for Covered Swap Entities, 76 Fed. Reg. 27,564 (May 11, 2011); Margin Requirements for Uncleared Swaps Dealers and Major Swap Participants, 76 Fed. Reg. 23,732 (Apr. 28, 2011).

from the IMF, have noted that an increase in central clearing of swaps may not, by itself, reduce risk and may increase risk.[98] Second, our indicators do not identify causal links between changes in swap market and the Dodd-Frank Act, including its regulations. Rather, the indicators begin to track changes in central clearing and collateralization in the swaps since the Dodd-Frank Act's passage to examine whether the changes are consistent with the act's swap reform goals for central clearing and collateralization.

Central Clearing Indicators

Federal financial regulators have reported that mandatory clearing through clearinghouses for certain swaps can reduce risk and provide other benefits. As noted by CFTC, central clearing mitigates counterparty risk to the extent that the clearinghouse is a more creditworthy counterparty relative to the original swap participants.[99] Clearinghouses have a variety of tools to monitor and manage counterparty risk, which include the contractual right to collect initial and variation margin associated with swap positions; issue margin calls whenever the margin in a customer's account has dropped below predetermined levels; and close out the swap positions of a customer that does not meet margin calls within a specified period. Further, to the extent that swap positions move from facing multiple counterparties in the OTC derivatives market to being run through a smaller number of clearinghouses, clearing may facilitate increased netting, which reduces operational risk and may reduce the amount of collateral that a counterparty must post or pay in terms of initial and variation margin. Although centralized clearing could remove a large portion of the interconnectedness of current OTC markets that leads to systemic risk, CFTC and others have noted that central clearing, by its nature, concentrates risk in a handful of entities.

We developed two complementary clearing indicators. Our first indicator measures the gross notional amount of swaps that are required to be cleared and are being cleared as a percentage of the gross notional amount of swaps required to be cleared.[100] This indicator shows the

---

[98]International Monetary Fund; *Global Financial Stability Report: Meeting New Challenges to Stability and Building a Safer System* (April 2010).

[99]See, for example, 77 Fed. Reg. 74,284 (Dec. 13, 2012).

[100]The gross notional amount is the nominal or face amount that is used to calculate payments made on swaps. This amount generally does not change hands and is thus referred to as notional.

progress being made by market participants in complying with any mandatory clearing requirement.[101] All else being equal, an increase in this indicator would be consistent with the act's swaps reforms. However, an increase in compliance with mandatory clearing requirements may not increase central clearing overall if market participants substitute away from swaps that are required to be cleared in favor of swaps that are not required to be cleared.[102] To assess the extent to which market participants are substituting away from swaps that are required to clear, we complement our first indicator with a second indicator that measures the gross notional amount of swaps that are required to be cleared (but are not necessarily cleared) as a percentage of the total gross notional amount of the swaps market. This indicator shows the share of the swap market comprised by swaps identified for mandatory clearing and helps determine the extent to which changes in the first indicator represent increases in central clearing overall.[103] For example, an increase in the first indicator—the percentage of swaps that are required to be cleared that are cleared—would indicate an increase in central clearing overall if the second indicator—the percentage of all swaps that are required to clear—does not decrease at the same time. In contrast, if the first indicator increases while the second decreases, then some of the increase in the first indicator likely is due to substitution away from swaps that are required to be cleared in favor of swaps that are not required to be cleared, which is not consistent with the act's swaps reforms.

Our indicators cover only the interest rate swaps and CDS markets, because only certain of these types of swaps are currently subject to CFTC's mandatory clearing requirement.[104] These are the two largest swaps markets. Based on CFTC's Swaps Report, the total gross notional amounts outstanding of the interest rate swap and CDS markets were about $419 trillion and $20 trillion, respectively, as of August 30, 2013.

---

[101]This indicator likely will be less than 100 percent because nonfinancial entities that use swaps to hedge or mitigate commercial risk are exempt from the clearing requirement.

[102]Market participants may also substitute away from swaps subject to a clearing mandate to centrally cleared futures contracts, and the overall percentage of centrally cleared swaps and futures contracts will not be captured by this indicator.

[103]This indicator likely will be less than 100 percent in part because some customized swaps will not be required to clear.

[104]As discussed, SEC has not yet subjected any security-based swaps to a mandatory clearing requirement.

The indicators are developed using data in the proposed version of CFTC's Swaps Report, which are estimates from a variety of sources that voluntarily submit the data.[105] CFTC's final version of its Swaps Report will use data collected in response to Dodd-Frank provisions, and CFTC staff stated that the agency was working to implement this transition.

Figure 2 shows the trends of our clearing indicators for interest rate swaps from January 2013 through August 2013. Our first indicator shows that market participants are making progress in meeting the clearing requirement: The percentage of swaps required to be cleared and that were cleared increased from around 53 percent to around 57 percent (based on gross notional amounts). Currently, not all interest rate swaps that are required to be cleared are being cleared, in part because CFTC is phasing in the requirement by staggering the compliance dates for different types of market participants and also because some nonfinancial entities that use swaps to hedge or mitigate commercial risk are exempt from the clearing requirement. The second indicator shows that interest rate swaps that are required to be cleared made up about 88 percent of the market (based on gross notional amount), and generally did not decrease during the period. This indicates that the increase in the first indicator represents an increase in central clearing that is consistent with the act's swaps reforms.

---

[105]Importantly, the data represent the global market and, according to CFTC staff, likely include swaps not under CFTC's regulatory jurisdiction. In addition, CFTC staff told us that the proposed version of the Swap Reports currently does not include data from one swap data repository. CFTC staff told us that the final version of the CFTC Swaps Report will represent only those swaps that are under CFTC's regulatory jurisdiction. In updating our clearing indicators in the future, we plan to use data from the final version of CFTC's Swap Report. If significant differences exist between the data in the proposed and final Swaps Reports, this year's indicators may not serve as a useful baseline, and we will make adjustments in future reports, as necessary and possible.

Figure 2: Trends in Central Clearing of Interest Rate Swaps (by Percentage of Gross Notional Value of Swaps), from January 2013 through August 2013

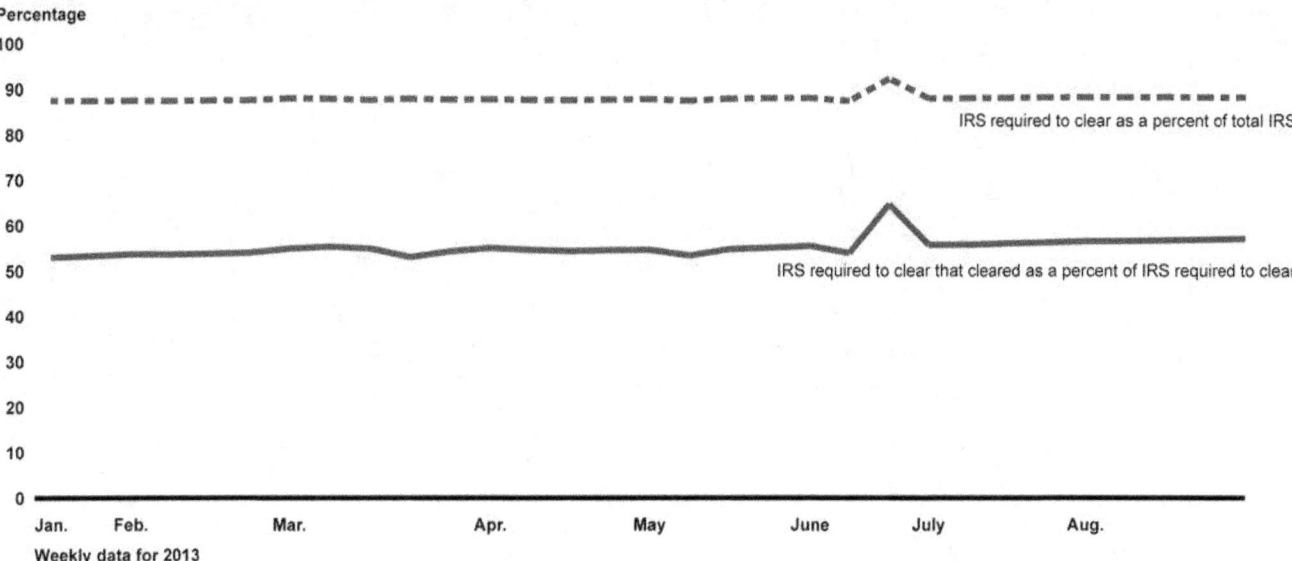

Source: GAO analysis of CFTC data.

Note: The types of interest rate swaps that are required to clear are fixed-to-floating rate swaps, basis swaps, forward rate agreements, and overnight index swaps. We used weekly data from CFTC Swaps Reports for the period from January 2, 2013, to August 28, 2013, to calculate (1) the gross notional amount of interest rate swaps that are required to clear and that actually cleared as a percentage of the gross notional amount of interest rate swaps that are required to clear and (2) the gross notional amount of interest rate swaps that are required to clear as a percentage of the total gross notional amount of interest rate swaps. In its rule requiring central clearing of interest rate swaps, CFTC set the earliest compliance date for March 2013. CFTC staff told us that they examined the rapid increase and decrease in the rate of central clearing of interest rate swaps on June 28, 2012 and July 5, 2012, respectively. CFTC staff told us that the change appeared to result largely from a decrease in uncleared interest rate swaps, and that they are looking further into the matter.

Figure 3 shows the trends of our two clearing indicators for CDSs from January 2013 through August 2013. Our first indicator shows that, based on gross notional amount, about 27 percent of swaps required to be cleared were cleared at the end of the period, compared to about 24 percent at the beginning of the period. The second indictor shows that, based on gross notional amount, CDSs required to be cleared accounted for about 35 percent of the market at the end of the period, compared to about 30 percent at the beginning of the period. This trend in the percentage of all CDSs that are required to clear is not consistent with market participants substituting away from CDSs that are required to clear in favor of CDSs that are not required to clear. It follows that the increase in the percentage of required-to-clear CDSs that cleared over the period generally is consistent with the act's swaps reforms.

Figure 3: Percentage of Credit Default Swaps Centrally Cleared (by Gross Notional Value of Swaps), from January 2013 through August 2013

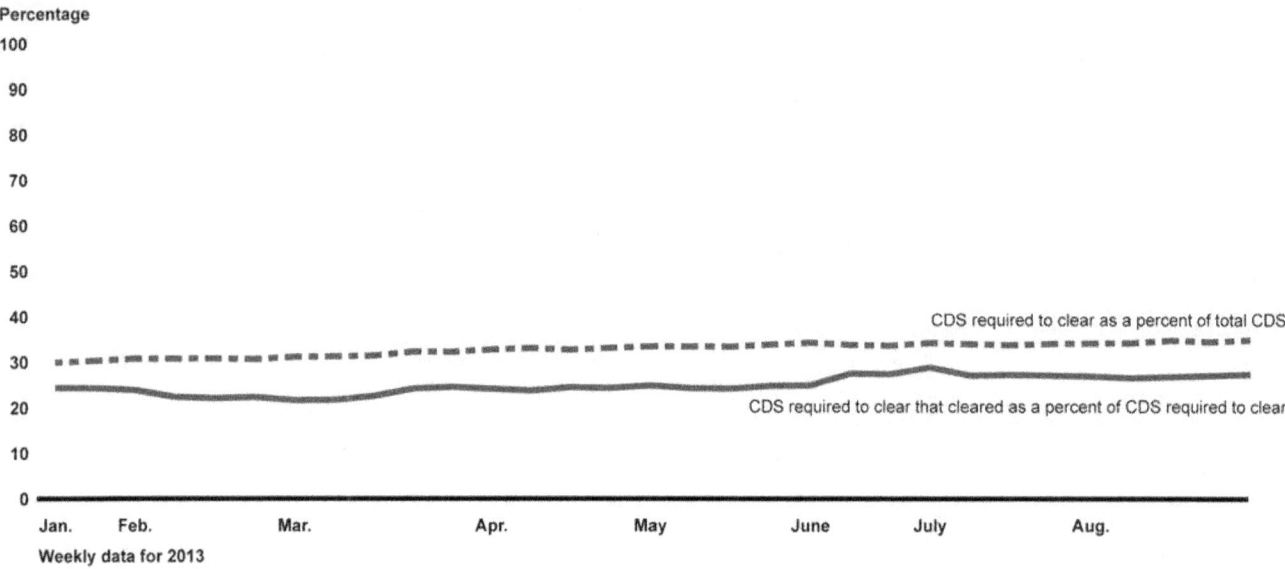

Source: GAO analysis of CFTC data.

Note: The types of credit default swaps that are required to clear are untranched European and North American index credit default swaps. We used weekly data from CFTC Swaps Reports for the period from January 2, 2013, to August 28, 2013, to calculate (1) the gross notional amount of credit default swaps that are required to clear and that actually cleared as a percentage of the gross notional amount of credit default swaps that are required to clear and (2) the gross notional amount of credit default swaps that are required to clear as a percentage of the total gross notional amount of credit default swaps. In its rule requiring central clearing of CDS, CFTC set the earliest compliance date for March 2013.

Margin Indicators

We developed a second set of indicators to measure changes in the collection of margin collateral for OTC derivatives.[106] The first margin indicator measures the fair value of collateral pledged by all counterparties to secure OTC derivatives contracts as a percentage of net current credit exposure to those counterparties for bank, financial, and savings and loan holding companies that reported positive credit

---

[106]Our indicators use data collected by the Federal Reserve on form FR Y-9C, which currently requires bank, financial, and savings and loan holding companies with more than $10 billion in assets to report their net current credit exposure to counterparties in OTC derivatives contracts and the fair value of the collateral pledged by those counterparties to secure the contracts.

exposure.[107] The second set of margin indicators measures collateral pledged by different types of counterparties—banks and securities firms, monoline financial guarantors, hedge funds, sovereign governments, and corporations and all other counterparties—as a percentage of credit exposure to different types of counterparties. The net current credit exposure approximates the credit loss that a bank, financial, or savings and loan holding company would suffer if its counterparties defaulted on their OTC derivatives contracts.[108] To protect itself from such a loss, a swap entity can require its counterparties to post margin collateral in an amount equal to or greater than the exposure of the contracts. An increase in these indicators would suggest that holding companies are requiring their counterparties to post a greater amount of collateral against their credit exposure due to derivatives contracts overall, which would be consistent with the purposes of the act's swap reforms.

Although CFTC, SEC, and the prudential regulators have not finalized their margin rules for uncleared swaps, figures 4 and 5 show the trends in our margin indicators from the second quarter of 2009 through the fourth quarter of 2012. Figure 4 shows that holding companies in our sample have increased the rate of collateralization of their net current credit exposure from OTC derivatives from 62 percent to 82 percent over the period, suggesting that these holding companies are requiring their counterparties to post a greater amount of collateral against their derivatives contracts. However, as discussed later, aggregate measures of collateralization rates can mask differences in collateralization rates for different counterparty types.

---

[107]The fair value of collateral is the amount that would be received if the collateral was sold in an orderly transaction between market participants in its principal market on the measurement date.

[108]Net current credit exposure to a counterparty is derived by first calculating the fair values of all derivative contracts with that counterparty, where the fair value of a derivative contract is analogous to the fair value of collateral. If a legally enforceable bilateral netting agreement is in place, the fair values of all applicable derivative contracts in the scope of the netting agreement with that counterparty are netted to a single amount, which may be positive, negative, or zero. Net current credit exposure across all counterparties is the sum of the gross positive fair values for counterparties without legal netting arrangements and the net current credit exposure for counterparties with legal netting agreements.

GAO-14-67 Dodd-Frank Regulations

Figure 4: Fair Value of Collateral as a Percentage of Net Current Credit Exposure from OTC Derivatives Contracts for All Counterparty Types Combined, from Second Quarter 2009 through Second Quarter 2013

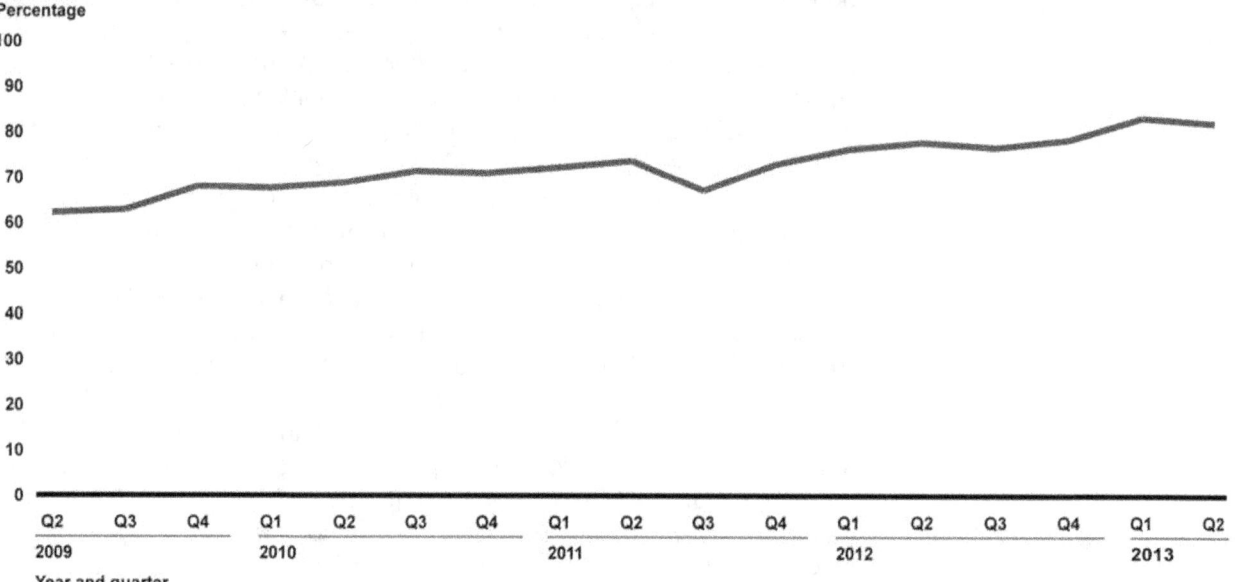

Source: GAO analysis of Federal Reserve Bank of Chicago data.

Note: To calculate the fair value of collateral as a percentage of net current credit exposure for all counterparty types, we used quarterly data on bank, financial, and savings and loan holding companies from form FR Y-9C for the period from second quarter 2009 to second quarter 2013. For each quarter, we used data for all holding companies that reported positive net current credit exposure to at least one type of counterparty, and we divided total fair value of collateral pledged by all counterparty types for all of these holding companies by total net current credit exposure to all counterparty types for all of these holding companies.

Figure 5 shows that the rate of collateralization of net current credit exposure from OTC derivatives has consistently differed by the type of counterparty, with hedge funds posting the most collateral as a percentage of credit exposure and sovereign governments typically posting the least. According to OCC, the rates differ, in part, because swap dealers may require certain counterparties, such as hedge funds, to post both initial and variation margin and other counterparties, such as banks and securities firms, to post only variation margin. Depending on how the margin rules are finalized, the rates of collateralization for some counterparties may increase.

GAO-14-67 Dodd-Frank Regulations

Figure 5: Fair Value of Collateral as a Percentage of Net Current Credit Exposure from OTC Derivatives Contracts by Counterparty Type, from Second Quarter 2009 through Second Quarter 2013

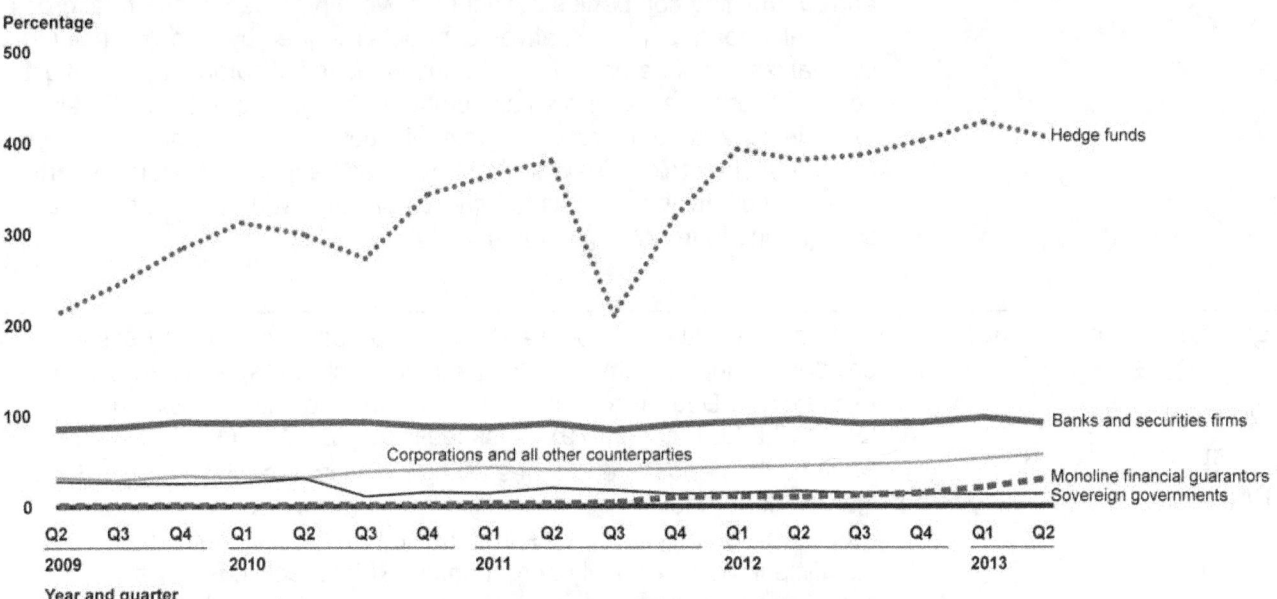

Source: GAO analysis of Federal Reserve Bank of Chicago data.

Note: To calculate the fair value of collateral as a percentage of net current credit exposure for each counterparty type, we used quarterly data on bank, financial, and savings and loan holding companies from form FR Y-9C for the period from second quarter 2009 to second quarter 2013. For each quarter and for each counterparty type, we used data for all holding companies that reported positive net current credit exposure to that counterparty type, and we divided total fair value of collateral pledged by that counterparty type for all of these holding companies by total net current credit exposure to that counterparty type for all of these holding companies.

Our margin indicators are subject to important limitations. First, both net current credit exposure and the fair value of collateral are as of a point in time because the fair values of derivatives contracts and collateral can fluctuate over time. Second, an average collateralization of 100 percent does not ensure that all current counterparty exposures have been eliminated, because one counterparty's credit exposures may be overcollateralized but another counterparty's credit exposure may be undercollateralized. Third, our indicators measure the fair value of the collateral held against net current credit exposures but do not necessarily measure the risk of uncollateralized losses. The fair value of net current credit exposure does not fully account for the riskiness of any single swap contract, so it is possible for the rate of collateralization to increase while the risk of uncollateralized losses also has increased, if a party has entered into riskier swaps. Fourth, there are over 1,000 holding companies in our sample, but less than 100 holding companies report positive credit exposure to counterparties in OTC derivatives contracts and five holding companies account for over 95 percent of the total gross notional amount of all derivatives contracts reported by all of the holding companies in our sample. Thus, trends in these indicators largely reflect collateralization rates for a small number of holding companies. Finally, these indicators do not reflect collateralization rates for companies, such as standalone broker-dealers, that have credit exposure to counterparties in OTC derivatives contracts but are not affiliated with a bank, financial, or savings and loan holding company.

Regulators Vary in Their Approaches and Progress in Developing Retrospective Review Plans

Federal financial regulators vary in their approaches and progress in developing and implementing plans to conduct retrospective reviews of their existing Dodd-Frank and other rules in recognition of Executive Order 13,579 (E.O. 13,579).[109] Issued in July 2011, E.O. 13,579 seeks to facilitate the periodic review of existing significant regulations by asking independent regulatory agencies to consider how best to promote retrospective analysis of rules that may be outmoded, ineffective, insufficient, or excessively burdensome. Retrospective reviews complement the prospective analysis that agencies conduct as part of their rulemaking (discussed above) and can provide insights on how regulations actually are working. E.O 13,579 represents the first time the President has issued an executive order to ask independent regulatory agencies to produce retrospective review plans for public scrutiny. But independent regulators, such as the federal financial regulators, are not required to follow this order.

Most federal financial regulators told us that they were not developing retrospective review plans specifically in response to E.O. 13,579. As a matter of policy or to satisfy statutory obligations, federal financial regulators generally had been conducting retrospective reviews before

---

[109]Exec. Order No. 13,579. 76 Fed. Reg. 41,587 (July 14, 2011). Section 2 of the order emphasizes the importance of retrospective analysis of rules. It contains a "look back" provision: "Within 120 days of the date of this order, each independent regulatory agency should develop and release to the public a plan, consistent with law and reflecting its resources and regulatory priorities and processes, under which the agency will periodically review its existing significant regulations to determine whether any such regulations should be modified, streamlined, expanded, or repealed so as to make the agency's regulatory program more effective or less burdensome in achieving the regulatory objectives."

the issuance of E.O. 13,579. In that regard, the prudential regulators told us that they generally view their retrospective rule reviews conducted in accordance with statute or policy to be consistent with the order's principles and objectives. For example, prudential regulators noted that the Economic Growth and Regulatory Paperwork Reduction Act of 1996 (EGRPRA) requires them to review their regulations at least once every 10 years and identify and eliminate any regulatory requirements that are outdated, unnecessary, or unduly burdensome.[110] The regulators reported on the results of their last EGRPRA review in July 2007, which was done over a 3-year period.[111] During the review, the regulators undertook various efforts to reduce regulatory burden on their supervised institutions, including by streamlining supervisory processes. They also identified four areas to explore further for opportunities to revise regulations: suspicious activity reports, lending limits, the Basel II capital framework, and consumer disclosures. The next EGRPRA review must be completed by 2016. Three prudential regulators told us that they are actively planning for the review. According to one prudential regulator, CFPB, the Federal Reserve, FDIC, NCUA, and OCC, are working in a collaborative fashion under the auspices of the Federal Financial Institutions Examination Council to develop a program to conduct a comprehensive review of the regulations under EGRPGRA. In addition, some prudential regulators have conducted periodic, retrospective reviews of their existing rules as a matter of policy or practice. For example, NCUA has a policy of reviewing one-third of its rules on an annual basis, and the Federal Reserve has a policy of reviewing each of its rules at least once every 5 years. FDIC is undertaking a review of its regulations to eliminate and reduce unnecessary regulatory burden in light of the regulations it incorporated when it took on supervision of state-charted thrifts upon the dissolution of the Office of Thrift Supervision. In addition, according to FDIC staff, the agency recently revised its policies, in part, to reaffirm its commitment to periodically undertake a review of each FDIC regulation and policy statement. Lastly, as part of its effort to integrate the Office of Thrift Supervision into its agency, OCC has been undertaking a comprehensive review of its and the Office of Thrift

---

[110]Pub. L. No. 104-208, Div. A, Tit. II, § 2222, 110 Stat. 3009-394, 3009-414 (1996) (codified at 12 U.S.C. § 3311).

[111]Joint Report to Congress July 31, 2007; Economic Growth and Regulatory Paperwork Reduction Act. 72 Fed. Reg. 62,036 (Nov. 1, 2007).

GAO-14-67 Dodd-Frank Regulations

Supervision's regulations to eliminate duplication and reduce unnecessary regulatory burden.

According to CFPB officials, the agency is not developing a retrospective review plan in response to E.O. 13,579 but, instead, is focusing on fulfilling its retrospective review requirements under section 1022 of the Dodd-Frank Act. Under the act, CFPB is required to assess retrospectively each significant rule or order adopted by CFPB under federal consumer financial law to address, among other things, the rule or order's effectiveness in meeting the act's purposes and goals. CFPB is required to publish a report of its assessment no later than 5 years after the rule or order's effective date, and is required to solicit public comment to inform its assessment. The officials said that they are in the initial stage of developing a review plan, which includes identifying what data will be needed and how such data can be collected, but have not yet drafted a plan. According to the officials, after the section 1022 reviews are completed and based on any lessons learned, CFPB may develop a plan pursuant to E.O. 13,579 to review its existing rules on a recurring basis. In a related effort, CFPB requested public comment in December 2011 on streamlining regulations it inherited from other federal agencies.[112] As a result of the comments received, CFPB has identified several priority areas for regulatory action.[113]

Only CFTC and SEC voluntarily developed retrospective review plans in response to the executive order. In a June 2011 request for information, CFTC outlined a two-phase plan to conduct periodic, retrospective reviews of its existing regulations.[114] Under the first phase, CFTC has examined and revised a number of its existing regulations as part of its

---

[112]76 Fed. Reg. 75,825 (Dec. 5. 2011).

[113]For example, in May 2013, CFPB issued a final rule amending the ability-to-pay regulations under the Credit Card Accountability Responsibility and Disclosure Act of 2009 in response to industry participants' comments to its December 2011 request. 78 Fed. Reg. 25,818 (May 3, 2013).

[114]76 Fed. Reg. 38,328 (June 30, 2011). CFTC's release responded to Executive Order 13,563, entitled "Improving Regulation and Regulatory Review," which supplements and reaffirms Executive Order 12,866 partly by incorporating its principles, structures, and definitions. Exec. Order 13,563, 76 Fed. Reg. 3821 (Jan. 18, 2011). Section 6 of the order focuses on the importance of maintaining a consistent culture of retrospective review and analysis by agencies of their regulatory programs. Shortly after the issuance of Executive Order 13,563, the President issued E.O. 13,579 to encourage independent regulatory agencies to comply with E.O. 13,563.

implementation of the Dodd-Frank Act. Under the second phase, CFTC plans to conduct retrospective reviews of the remainder of its regulations after substantial completion of its Dodd-Frank rulemakings. CFTC has provided OMB with periodic status reports on its retrospective review plan and reported in July 2013 that it still is in phase one. In a September 2011 request for information, SEC requested public comments to assist it in developing a retrospective review plan as part of its ongoing efforts to update its regulations and in light of E.O. 13,579.[115] At the same time, SEC noted that it has formal and informal processes for reviewing existing rules to assess their continued utility and effectiveness.[116] According to SEC staff, they have reviewed public comments received in response to the release and worked on a draft plan, but the agency has not yet approved or issued a final plan.

In July 2011, OMB issued guidance on E.O. 13,579 and noted that each agency should exercise its discretion to develop a retrospective review plan tailored to its specific mission, resources, organizational structure, and rulemaking history and volume.[117] According to the guidance, each agency should set its own priorities, but its retrospective review plans might address the following five topics. As federal financial regulators vary in the development and implementation of their retrospective review plans, they also vary in the extent to which they address or plan to address the topics outlined in OMB's guidance.

- **Public participation.** Per OMB's guidance, agencies should solicit the views of the public on how best to promote retrospective analysis of rules. Even before plans are written, for example, the public might be asked to provide comments on how such plans might be devised and to help identify those rules that might be modified, streamlined, expanded, or repealed. Regulators generally have sought public input or plan to seek public input about their retrospective review plans. In their *Federal Register* releases, CFTC and SEC requested public comments on various aspects of their plans. Under the EGRPRA review, the prudential regulators are required under EGRPRA to

---

[115]76 Fed. Reg. 56,128 (Sept.12, 2011).

[116]For example, SEC noted that it retrospectively reviews rules based on suggestions from investors, investor and industry groups, and others and as required by section 610(a) of the Regulatory Flexibility Act.

[117]M-11-28 (July 22, 2011).

categorize regulations by type and seek public comment on them. According to FDIC staff, prudential regulators currently are discussing how best to obtain public input for the EGRPRA process. Each year, NCUA invites the public to comment on the rules proposed for review that year. Also, CFPB is required to solicit public comment to inform its statutorily required retrospective reviews.

- **Prioritization.** Per OMB's guidance, the plan should specify factors that the agency will consider and the process that the agency will use in setting priorities and selecting rules for review. To the extent feasible, the plan should also include an initial list of candidate rules for review over the next two years, with clear timelines and deadlines. Regulators generally have not specified the factors that they will use to prioritize and select rules for review but have indicated that they plan to do so. CFTC and SEC asked for public comments on the factors they should use to prioritize and select rules for review. In its plan, CFTC noted that its Regulatory Review Group, consisting of senior staff, will recommend to the CFTC Commission a list of candidate rules for review, in part based on public comments. Under the EGRPRA review, the prudential regulators are required to categorize regulations by type and seek public comment on them to identify regulatory areas that are outdated, unnecessary, or unduly burdensome. According to FDIC staff, prudential regulators are developing a plan to efficiently and effectively complete the EGRPRA review process. Lastly, CFPB's review under the Dodd-Frank Act must cover all of its significant rules, and NCUA's review covers one-third of the agency's rules annually.

- **Analysis of costs and benefits.** Per OMB's guidance, agencies may find it useful to engage in a retrospective analysis of the costs and benefits (both quantitative and qualitative) of regulations chosen for review. The guidance suggests that the plan may address the metrics that the agency will use to evaluate regulations after they have been implemented, and the steps the agency has taken to ensure that it has high-quality data and robust models with which to conduct retrospective analyses. Regulators generally have not yet specified the metrics they will use to evaluate regulations or steps to be taken to ensure that they have high-quality data with which to conduct their retrospective analysis. SEC asked for public comments on, among other things, how it can obtain and consider data and analyses to assess the benefits of its rules. Likewise, CFPB officials told us that they are exploring what data they may collect to analyze their rules.

- **Structure and staffing.** Per OMB's guidance, responsibility for retrospective review should be vested with a high-level agency official who can secure cooperation across the agency. The plan should also consider how best to maintain sufficient independence from the offices responsible for writing and implementing regulations. Finally, the plan should identify possible actions to strengthen internal review expertise, if necessary. Regulators generally expect their office of general counsel or other nonrulemaking group to be responsible for overseeing implementation of their plans. For example, SEC has indicated that its Division of Economic and Risk Analysis will conduct the retrospective evaluations, and CFTC plans to form a group of senior staff that will implement its retrospective review plan. CFPB officials told us that the agency's research group likely will oversee the reviews. NCUA's Office of General Counsel conducts the agency's retrospective reviews.

- **Coordination with other forms of retrospective analysis and review.** Per OMB's guidance, many independent agencies already are engaged in retrospective analysis and review under existing requirements and authorities. The guidance states that it is appropriate to use existing processes and information as significant inputs into plans. As discussed, prudential regulators are using their existing retrospective reviews in lieu of developing specific retrospective review plans in response to E.O. 13,579.

Revisiting their retrospective analyses of their Dodd-Frank regulations after the regulations are implemented will allow regulators to determine whether regulations are achieving their intended purpose without creating unintended consequences that negatively impact the markets. Such reviews can also signal whether changes should be made to the existing rules to better achieve their intended purposes. In our prior work, we identified procedures and practices that could be particularly helpful in improving the effectiveness of retrospective reviews.[118] In particular, we noted that agencies would be better prepared to undertake reviews if they had identified the needed data before beginning a review and, even better, before promulgating the rule. If agencies fail to plan for how they will measure the performance of their rules and how they will obtain the data they need to do so, they may be limited in their ability to accurately measure the progress or true effect of the regulations. In that regard, we recommended in our prior report that the federal financial regulators develop plans that determine how they will measure the impact of Dodd-Frank regulations—for example, determining how and when to collect, analyze, and report needed data.[119] To date, regulators have not

---

[118]See GAO, *Reexamining Regulations: Opportunities Exist to Improve Effectiveness and Transparency of Retrospective Reviews*, GAO-07-791 (Washington, D.C.: July 16, 2007).

[119]See GAO-12-151.

implemented our recommendation. We maintain that doing so would position them to make their future retrospective reviews as robust as possible.

Conclusions

Federal financial regulators have considerable work under way to implement the Dodd-Frank Act reforms that could improve the U.S. financial system in many ways. However, much work remains to implement the reforms. For example, many rulemakings are yet to be finalized. Moreover, completing the rulemaking process does not mean that reforms are fully implemented. Rather, it will take time—beyond the time spent on finalizing the rulemakings—for regulators and industry to adopt the reforms contained in the rulemakings, and even longer to determine the actual effect of the reforms.

To date, OMB, in consultation with federal agencies, has classified 36 of the Dodd-Frank rules as major under CRA and, thus, expects them to have a large effect on the economy. As provided by CRA, these rules could not take effect until the later of 60 days after Congress receives the rule report, or 60 days after the rule is published in the *Federal Register*, as long as Congress does not pass a joint resolution of disapproval. OMB provided guidance on implementing CRA in 1999, but such guidance does not establish standardized processes for submitting rules to OMB for its review or applying CRA's criteria. In the absence of such guidance, we found that federal financial regulators may have used different processes for submitting their rules and analyses to OMB, and for applying CRA criteria. These inconsistent processes could lead to the inconsistent classification of some rules. To the extent that any major rules are not being classified as such, those rules would not be subject to the 60-day congressional notice required under CRA before major rules become effective.

Recommendations for Executive Action

To help ensure that OMB, in consultation with federal financial regulators, consistently classifies Dodd-Frank rules as major under CRA, we recommend that the Director of OMB, through the Administrator of the Office of Information and Regulatory Affairs, issue additional guidance to help standardize processes for identifying major rules under CRA, including on (1) the extent to which agencies should submit rules to OMB for review, such as whether agencies should submit only those rules their analyses indicate are major or all rules, and (2) how agencies should apply CRA's major rule criteria in their analyses, such as whether agencies should include indirect benefits or costs, combine benefits or costs of separate but related rules, or aggregate benefits or costs for jointly issued rules.

Agency Comments and Our Evaluation

We provided a draft of this report to CFPB, CFTC, FDIC, the Federal Reserve Board, FSOC, NCUA, OMB, OCC, SEC, and Treasury for review and comment. CFPB, CFTC, FDIC, the Federal Reserve Board, FSOC, OMB, OCC, SEC, and Treasury provided technical comments, which we have incorporated, as appropriate. Treasury (on behalf of FSOC) and NCUA provided written comments that we have reprinted in appendixes IX and X, respectively. In its comment letter, Treasury noted that FSOC has taken a variety of actions to facilitate coordination and consultation among financial regulators, such as through its deputies and functional committees, and continually seeks ways to further enhance collaboration. We describe these actions in the draft report. In its letter, NCUA agreed with our findings, conclusions, and recommendation.

OMB staff provided comments on a draft of our report via e-mail through their GAO liaison on November 25, 2013. In those comments, OMB disagreed with our findings and recommendation concerning OMB's application of the major rule criteria under CRA. Specifically, OMB disagreed with our findings that OMB inconsistently applied CRA criteria in its designation of major rules and stated that the examples in our draft report are not actual inconsistencies in the application of the CRA criteria. In addition, OMB noted that two of our examples reflected a challenge faced by OMB in determining whether a rule is major. Specifically, agencies often do not have the data needed to conduct a precise analysis of a rule's economic impact but, nevertheless, will recommend that a rule be designated as major if their analysis strongly suggests that the rule may be major. OMB said that in these circumstances, it generally will rely on an agency's expert judgment and concur with its recommendation. Furthermore, OMB said that even if some rule determinations under CRA were inconsistent, such outcomes may not result in any real-world consequence. For example, a rule incorrectly determined to be non-major under CRA could have an effective date less than 60 days after the rule's submission to Congress, but only if the agency did not plan to set the rule's effective date 60 or more days after the rule's submission. Finally, given these concerns, OMB questioned what new guidance to agencies would entail. Therefore, OMB suggested eliminating the recommendation from the draft report.

We maintain that the findings and recommendation on the major rule designation process are appropriate. First, we did not seek to determine whether any of the individual rules we reviewed were misclassified under CRA. Instead, our analysis identified examples in which federal agencies used different processes (1) for submitting their rules and supporting analyses to OMB and (2) in applying the CRA major rule criteria, which we concluded could lead to inconsistent classifications of similar rules under CRA. Indeed, determining whether any of the rules we reviewed actually were misclassified is not possible without clear guidance on whether agencies, for example, may consider a rule's indirect consequences, combine similar rules, or add a rule's benefits and costs in developing their designation recommendation. Our recommendation serves to address this gap in guidance and help ensure more standardized processes. We clarified a heading in the draft report to reflect our focus on the processes used by OMB and federal financial regulators.

Second, we agree that federal financial regulators face challenges in quantifying the benefits and costs of their rules and have highlighted such challenges in our prior reports.[120] However, again, our findings and recommendation focus on inconsistencies in the processes used by OMB and federal financial regulators to designate major rules under CRA—not on the analyses conducted by the regulators.

Third, CRA gives Congress 60 days to review a major rule before the rule can become effective, during which time Congress can issue a joint resolution disapproving the rule. While OMB notes that there might not be a real-world consequence if a rule is misclassified as non-major, this outcome relies on the issuing agency setting an effective date for the rule of at least 60 days after a rule's submission to Congress. Moreover, such a misclassification could infringe upon Congress's ability to reject the rule. Additionally, under CRA, GAO is required to provide Congress with a report on each major rule that contains GAO's assessment of each issuing agency's compliance with the procedural steps required by various acts and executive orders, including preparation of a cost-benefit analysis. In its mandated annual reports to Congress discussing the benefits and costs of federal regulations, OMB has stated that it uses GAO major rule reports as the sole source of information for analyzing

---

[120]GAO-12-151 and GAO-13-101.

major rules issued by independent regulatory agencies.[121] A misclassification of a major rule as non-major would mean that information on that rule would not be highlighted to Congress and the public in a GAO report and would, in turn, not be considered in OMB's annual reports to Congress on the benefits and costs of federal regulations.

Finally, although OMB issued guidance to federal agencies in 1999 on implementing CRA, the guidance did not clearly articulate the processes agencies should use to (1) submit their rules and analysis to OMB or (2) apply the CRA major rule criteria. In the absence of such guidance, we found that federal financial regulators varied in the processes they used to submit rules and analysis to OMB and their application of CRA criteria. For example, as we discuss in the report, SEC and CFPB staff told us that they did not know whether they were permitted to add costs and benefits or combine rules, respectively, in assessing whether a rule was major. In that regard, we maintain that additional guidance on the processes we identified would enhance the ability of OMB and federal financial regulators to fulfill their responsibilities under CRA.

We are sending copies of this report to CFPB, CFTC, FDIC, the Federal Reserve Board, FSOC, NCUA, OMB, OCC, SEC, Treasury, interested congressional committees and members, and others. This report will also be available at no charge on our website at http://www.gao.gov.

---

[121]OMB is required to produce annual reports to Congress on the benefits and costs of federal regulations. Consolidated Appropriations Act of 2001, Pub. L. No. 106-554, § 624, 114 Stat. 2763, 2763A-161 (2000) (codified at 31 U.S.C. § 1105 note). See, for example, OMB, *2013 Draft Report to Congress on the Benefits and Costs of Federal Regulations and Agency Compliance with the Unfunded Mandates Reform Act* (Washington, D.C: 2013); and OMB, *2012 Report to Congress on the Benefits and Costs of Federal Regulations and Unfunded Mandates on State, Local, and Tribal Entities* (Washington, D.C: 2012).

Should you or your staff have questions concerning this report, please contact me at (202) 512-8678 or clowersa@gao.gov. Contact points for our Offices of Congressional Relations and Public Affairs may be found on the last page of this report. Key contributors to this report are listed in appendix XI.

A. Nicole Clowers
Director Financial Markets and Community Investment

List of Addressees

The Honorable Harry Reid
Majority Leader
The Honorable Mitch McConnell
Minority Leader
United States Senate

The Honorable John Boehner
Speaker
The Honorable Nancy Pelosi
Minority Leader
House of Representatives

The Honorable Debbie Stabenow
Chairwoman
The Honorable Thad Cochran
Ranking Member
Committee on Agriculture, Nutrition and Forestry
United States Senate

The Honorable Barbara A. Mikulski
Chairwoman
The Honorable Richard Shelby
Vice Chairman
Committee on Appropriations
United States Senate

The Honorable Tim Johnson
Chairman
The Honorable Michael Crapo
Ranking Member
Committee on Banking, Housing, and Urban Affairs
United States Senate

The Honorable John D. Rockefeller IV
Chairman
The Honorable John Thune
Ranking Member
Committee on Commerce, Science, and Transportation
United States Senate

The Honorable Frank D. Lucas
Chairman
The Honorable Collin C. Peterson
Ranking Member
Committee on Agriculture
House of Representatives

The Honorable Harold Rogers
Chairman
The Honorable Nita Lowey
Ranking Member
Committee on Appropriations
House of Representatives

The Honorable Fred Upton
Chairman
The Honorable Henry A. Waxman
Ranking Member
Committee on Energy and Commerce
House of Representatives

The Honorable Jeb Hensarling
Chairman
The Honorable Maxine Waters
Ranking Member
Committee on Financial Services
House of Representatives

Appendix I: Objectives, Scope, and Methodology

This report examines rulemaking under the Dodd-Frank Wall Street Reform and Consumer Protection Act of 2010 (Dodd-Frank Act). More specifically, we examined (1) the regulatory analysis conducted by federal agencies in their Dodd-Frank rulemakings, including their assessments of which rules they considered to be major rules under the Congressional Review Act (CRA); (2) interagency coordination by the agencies in their Dodd-Frank rulemakings and by the Consumer Financial Protection Bureau (CFPB) with other agencies in connection to its supervision of large banks and certain nonbank financial service providers; and (3) possible impact of selected Dodd-Frank provisions and their implementing regulations and agency plans to assess such regulations retrospectively.[1]

To examine the regulatory analyses and coordination conducted by the regulators, we focused our analysis on final rules issued pursuant to the Dodd-Frank Act that became effective from July 24, 2012, through July 22, 2013, a total of 70 rules (see app. II). To identify these rules, we used a website maintained by the Federal Reserve Bank of St. Louis that tracks Dodd-Frank regulations.[2] We corroborated the data with officials from the agencies under review.

In examining the regulatory analyses of the federal agencies in our review, we reviewed federal statutes, regulations, GAO studies, and other material to identify the regulatory analyses, including benefit-cost analysis, required to be conducted by the federal agencies as part of their Dodd-Frank rulemakings. Of the 70 rules within our scope, 59 rules were substantive regulations— generally subject to public notice and comment

---

[1]The agencies covered in our review are the federal financial regulators, the Financial Stability Oversight Council, and the Department of the Treasury. We use the term "federal financial regulators" to refer to the Consumer Financial Protection Bureau, Commodity Futures Trading Commission, Federal Deposit Insurance Corporation, Federal Reserve, Office of the Comptroller of the Currency, National Credit Union Administration, and Securities and Exchange Commission.

[2]In this report, we use the terms "rules," "regulations," or "rulemakings" generally to refer to *Federal Register* notices of agency action pursuant to the Dodd-Frank Act, including regulations, interpretive rules, general statements of policy, guidance, and rules that deal with agency organization, procedure, or practice. Combined with our past two reports, we have reviewed all Dodd-Frank Act rules in effect as of July 22, 2013. See GAO, *Dodd-Frank Act Regulations: Implementation Could Benefit from Additional Analyses and Coordination*, GAO-12-151 (Washington, D.C.: Nov. 10, 2011), and *Dodd-Frank Act Regulations: Agencies' Efforts to Analyze and Coordinate Their Rules*, GAO-13-101 (Washington, D.C.: Dec. 18, 2012).

under the Administrative Procedure Act—and required the agencies to
conduct some form of regulatory analysis.[3] For each of the 59 rules, we
reviewed final rule *Federal Register* releases to document and summarize
the analyses conducted by the regulators under review. Using GAO's
Federal Rules database we found that 10 of the 59 rules were classified
by the Office of Management and Budget (OMB), in consultation with the
rulemaking agencies, as major rules under CRA (that is, have resulted in
or are likely to result in an annual impact on the economy of $100 million
or more, a major increase in costs or prices, or significant adverse effects
on competition, employment, investment, productivity, innovation, or on
the ability of U.S.-based enterprises to compete with foreign-based
enterprises in domestic and export markets). For agencies subject to
Executive Order 12,866 (E.O. 12,866), such major rules would be
considered significant regulatory actions and subject to formal benefit-
cost analysis.[4] We developed a data collection instrument to compare
and assess the regulatory analysis conducted for the 10 major rules
against the principles outlined in OMB Circular A-4, which provides
guidance to federal agencies on the development of regulatory analysis.[5]
To conduct our analyses, we reviewed *Federal Register* releases of the
proposed and final rules. To examine how OMB, in consultation with
federal agencies, classifies rules as major, we reviewed CRA, GAO
reports, and other material. Rather than limiting our scope to major rules
effective from July 24, 2012, through July 22, 2013, we reviewed and
analyzed all final Dodd-Frank rules classified as major as of July 22,
2013. To identify such major rules, we relied on GAO's Federal Rules
database.[6] We identified 36 major rules issued pursuant to the Dodd-

---

[3]The other 11 rules were technical amendments to previous rules, general statements of
policy, interpretations, or guidance.

[4]CRA's definition of a major rule is similar, but not identical, to the definition of a
"significant regulatory action" under E.O. 12,866.

[5]As independent regulatory agencies that are not required to follow the economic analysis
requirements of E.O. 12,866, the financial regulators also are not required to follow OMB
Circular A-4. However, Circular A-4 is an example of best practices for agencies to follow
when conducting regulatory analyses, and the financial regulators have told us that they
follow the guidance in spirit.

[6]CRA requires agencies to file rules with Congress and the Comptroller General before
the rules can become effective. 5 U.S.C. § 801(a)(1)(A). To compile information on all the
rules submitted under CRA, GAO established a database and created a standardized
submission form to allow more consistent information collection. The Federal Rules
database is publicly available at www.gao.gov under Legal Decisions & Bid Protests.

Frank Act (which includes the 10 major rules mentioned above) and
corroborated our list with federal agencies under review. To examine the
basis for classifying the rules as major, we reviewed the impact analyses
prepared by the agencies and provided to OMB, if available; GAO reports
on major rules; and *Federal Register* releases on the rules. We also
interviewed officials from OMB and federal agencies about the processes
used to classify major rules.

To examine interagency coordination among the regulators, we reviewed
the Dodd-Frank Act, *Federal Register* releases, and GAO reports to
identify the interagency coordination or consultation requirements for the
70 Dodd-Frank rules within our scope. We also interviewed officials or
staff from the Commodity Futures Trading Commission (CFTC), CFPB,
and the Securities and Exchange Commission (SEC) to identify which
rules were subject to interagency coordination requirements under Titles
VII and X of the act. We found evidence of coordination between the
rulemaking agency and other regulators for 49 of the 70 regulations that
we reviewed. We reviewed the *Federal Register* releases of the proposed
and final rules and interviewed agency officials to document whether the
agencies coordinated or consulted with other U.S., foreign, or
international regulators, as required by the Dodd-Frank Act or on a
voluntary basis. To examine steps taken by CFPB to comply with the
act's interagency coordination and information-sharing requirements for
its supervision activities, we reviewed the act; CFPB's *Supervision and
Examination Manual*, memorandums of understanding with federal and
state regulators on interagency coordination, and other agency
documents; and GAO reports. We also interviewed officials from CFPB
and federal prudential regulators about their coordination with each other
and coordination challenges.

Finally, we took a multipronged approach to analyze what is known about
the impact of the Dodd-Frank Act on the financial marketplace. First, we
used bank holding company data from the Federal Reserve Bank of
Chicago (from FR Y-9C), Bureau of Economic Analysis, and Federal
Reserve Board's National Information Center, to update our indicators
monitoring changes in certain characteristics of systemically important
financial institutions (SIFI) that might be affected by Dodd-Frank

regulations.[7] Although changes in the indicators may be suggestive of the impact of the act on SIFIs, the indicators have a number of limitations, including that they do not identify any causal linkages between the act and changes in the indicators. Moreover, factors other than the act affect SIFIs and, thus, the indicators. Second, we used the Federal Reserve Bank of Chicago data to update our economic analysis estimating changes in the (1) cost of credit provided by bank SIFIs and (2) safety and soundness of bank SIFIs. Our analysis does not differentiate the effects of the act from simultaneous changes in economic conditions or other factors that may affect such companies. Third, the Dodd-Frank Act requires CFTC, SEC, and the prudential regulators to implement new reforms for swaps and security-based swaps to reduce risk, increase transparency, and improve market integrity. For example, the act provides for the registration of swap dealers, including subjecting them to minimum margin requirements, and authorizes CFTC and SEC to impose mandatory clearing requirements on swaps. We developed margin and clearing indicators that may reflect the act's impact on these activities using bank holding company data from the Federal Reserve Bank of Chicago (from FR Y-9C) and CFTC's Swaps Report, respectively. As new data become available, we expect to update and, as warranted, revise our indicators and create additional indicators to cover other provisions. Although changes in our indicators may be suggestive of the act's impact on the swaps market, the indicators have a number of limitations, including that they do not identify causal linkages between the act and changes in the indicators. Fourth, to assess agency plans to conduct retrospective reviews of their existing rules, we reviewed executive orders, including E.O. 13,579 that asks independent regulatory agencies to prepare retrospective review plans; OMB guidance; *Federal Register* releases, policies, and other agency documents pertaining to retrospective reviews; and GAO reports. Finally, we interviewed federal financial regulators about their plans to conduct retrospective reviews of their Dodd-Frank rules. For parts of our methodology that involved the

---

[7]The Dodd-Frank Act does not use the term "systemically important financial institution" (SIFI). This term is commonly used by academics and other experts to refer to bank holding companies with $50 billion or more in total consolidated assets and nonbank financial companies designated by the Financial Stability Oversight Council (FSOC) for Federal Reserve supervision and enhanced prudential standards under the Dodd-Frank Act. For purposes of this report, we refer to these bank and nonbank financial companies as bank systemically important financial institutions (bank SIFIs) and nonbank systemically important financial institutions (nonbank SIFIs), respectively. We also refer to nonbank SIFIs and bank SIFIs collectively as SIFIs when appropriate.

analysis of computer-processed data, we assessed the reliability of these data and determined that they were sufficiently reliable for our purposes.

We conducted this performance audit from January 2013 to December 2013 in accordance with generally accepted government auditing standards. Those standards require that we plan and perform the audit to obtain sufficient, appropriate evidence to provide a reasonable basis for our findings and conclusions based on our audit objectives. We believe that the evidence obtained provides a reasonable basis for our findings and conclusions based on our audit objectives.

Appendix II: Dodd-Frank Rules Effective as of July 22, 2013

The following table lists the Dodd-Frank rules that we identified as effective during the scope period for this review—July 24, 2012, through July 22, 2013.

Table 4: Dodd-Frank Rules Effective from July 24, 2012, through July 22, 2013

Rulemaking	Responsible regulator	Published date	Effective date[a]	Agency stated it conducted analysis required under		
				Regulatory Flexibility Act	Paperwork Reduction Act	Executive Order or statute[b]
Electronic Fund Transfers (Regulation E)	CFPB	2/7/2012	2/7/2013	Y	Y	Y
Customer Clearing Documentation, Timing of Acceptance for Clearing, and Clearing Member Risk Management	CFTC	4/9/2012	10/1/2012	Y	Y	Y
Guidance on the Effective Date of Section 716 of the Dodd-Frank Wall Street Reform and Consumer Protection Act	FDIC, FRS, and OCC	5/10/2012	7/16/2013	N/A	N/A	N/A
Swap Data Recordkeeping and Reporting Requirements: Pre-Enactment and Transition Swaps	CFTC	6/12/2012	8/13/2012	Y	Y	Y
Guidance on Due Diligence Requirements in Determining Whether Securities Are Eligible for Investment	OCC	6/13/2012	1/1/2013	N/A	N/A	N/A
Core Principles and Other Requirements for Designated Contract Markets	CFTC	6/19/2012	8/20/2012	Y	Y	Y
Listing Standards for Compensation Committees	SEC	6/27/2012	7/27/2012	Y	Y	Y
Confidential Treatment of Privileged Information	CFPB	7/5/2012	8/6/2012	Y	N/A	Y
Process for Submissions for Review of Security-Based Swaps for Mandatory Clearing and Notice Filing Requirements for Clearing Agencies; Technical Amendments to Rule 19b–4 and Form 19b–4 Applicable to All Self-Regulatory Organizations	SEC	7/13/2012	8/13/2012	Y	Y	Y
End-User Exception to the Clearing Requirement for Swaps	CFTC	7/19/2012	9/17/2012	Y	Y	Y
Defining Larger Participants of the Consumer Reporting Market	CFPB	7/20/2012	9/30/2012	Y	Y	Y
Swap Transaction Compliance and Implementation Schedule: Clearing Requirement Under Section 2(h) of the CEA	CFTC	7/30/2012	9/28/2012	Y	Y	Y
Financial Market Utilities	FRS	8/2/2012	9/14/2012	Y	Y	N/A
Debit Card Interchange Fees and Routing	FRS	8/3/2012	10/1/2012	Y	Y	N/A

Rulemaking	Responsible regulator	Published date	Effective date[a]	Agency stated it conducted analysis required under		
				Regulatory Flexibility Act	Paperwork Reduction Act	Executive Order or statute[b]
Further Definition of "Swap," "Security-Based Swap," and "Security-Based Swap Agreement"; Mixed Swaps; Security-Based Swap Agreement Recordkeeping	CFTC and SEC	8/13/2012	10/12/2012	Y	Y	Y
Electronic Fund Transfers (Regulation E)	CFPB	8/20/2012	2/7/2013	Y	Y	Y
Registration of Intermediaries	CFTC	8/28/2012	10/29/2012	Y	Y	Y
Risk-Based Capital Guidelines: Market Risk	FDIC, FRS, and OCC	8/30/2012	1/1/2013	Y	Y	N/A
Amendments to Commodity Pool Operator and Commodity Trading Advisor Regulations Resulting From the Dodd-Frank Act	CFTC	9/5/2012	11/5/2012	Y	Y	Y
Confirmation, Portfolio Reconciliation, Portfolio Compression, and Swap Trading Relationship Documentation Requirements for Swap Dealers and Major Swap Participants	CFTC	9/11/2012	11/13/2012	Y	Y	Y
Conflict Minerals	SEC	9/12/2012	11/13/2012	Y	Y	Y
Disclosure of Payments by Resource Extraction Issuersc	SEC	9/12/2012	11/13/2012	Y	Y	Y
Annual Stress Test	OCC	10/9/2012	10/9/2012	Y	Y	N/A
Supervisory and Company-Run Stress Test Requirements for Covered Companies	FRS	10/12/2012	11/15/2012	Y	Y	N/A
Annual Company-Run Stress Test Requirements for Banking Organizations With Total Consolidated Assets Over $10 Billion Other Than Covered Companies	FRS	10/12/2012	11/15/2012	Y	Y	N/A
Annual Stress Test	FDIC	10/15/2012	10/15/2012	Y	Y	N/A
Enforcement of Subsidiary and Affiliate Contracts by the FDIC as Receiver of a Covered Financial Company	FDIC	10/16/2012	11/15/2012	Y	Y	N/A
Swap Data Repositories: Interpretative Statement Regarding the Confidentiality and Indemnification Provisions of the Commodity Exchange Act	CFTC	10/25/2012	10/25/2012	N/A	N/A	N/A
Assessments, Large Bank Pricing	FDIC	10/31/2012	4/1/2013	Y	Y	N/A
Defining Larger Participants of the Consumer Debt Collection Market	CFPB	10/31/2012	1/2/2013	Y	Y	Y
Clearing Agency Standards	SEC	11/2/2012	1/2/2013	Y	Y	Y
Adaptation of Regulations To Incorporate Swaps	CFTC	11/2/2012	1/2/2013	Y	Y	Y

Rulemaking	Responsible regulator	Published date	Effective date[a]	Agency stated it conducted analysis required under		
				Regulatory Flexibility Act	Paperwork Reduction Act	Executive Order or statute[b]
Determination of Foreign Exchange Swaps and Foreign Exchange Forwards Under the Commodity Exchange Act	Treasury	11/20/2012	11/20/2012	Y	Y	Y
Truth in Lending (Regulation Z)[d]	CFPB and FRS	11/21/2012	1/1/2013	N/A	Y	N/A
Consumer Leasing (Regulation M)[d]	CFPB and FRS	11/21/2012	1/1/2013	N/A	Y	N/A
Truth in Lending (Regulation Z)	CFPB	11/21/2012	1/1/2013	N/A	N/A	N/A
Purchase of Certain Debt Securities by Business and Industrial Development Companies Relying on an Investment Company Act Exemption	SEC	11/23/2012	12/24/2012	Y	Y	Y
Delayed Implementation of Certain New Mortgage Disclosures	CFPB	11/23/2012	11/23/2012	Y	Y	Y
Alternatives to the Use of Credit Ratings	NCUA	12/13/2012	6/11/2013	Y	Y	N/A
Clearing Requirement Determination Under Section 2(h) of the CEA	CFTC	12/13/2012	2/11/2013	Y	Y	Y
Community Reinvestment Act Regulations[d]	FDIC, FRS, and OCC	12/21/2012	1/1/2013	N/A	Y	N/A
Adaptation of Regulations To Incorporate Swaps—Records of Transactions	CFTC	12/21/2012	2/19/2013	Y	Y	Y
Lending Limits[d]	OCC	12/31/2012	12/31/2012	N/A	Y	N/A
Final Exemptive Order Regarding Compliance with Certain Swap Regulations	CFTC	1/7/2013	12/21/2012	N/A	Y	Y
Transition Period Under Section 716 of the Dodd-Frank Wall Street Reform and Consumer Protection Act	OCC	1/8/2013	1/8/2013	N/A	N/A	N/A
Treasury Tax and Loan Depositaries; Depositaries and Financial Agents of the Government	NCUA	1/18/2013	1/18/2013	Y	Y	N/A
Escrow Requirements Under the Truth in Lending Act (Regulation Z)	CFPB	1/22/2013	6/1/2013	Y	Y	Y
Lost Securityholders and Unresponsive Payees	SEC	1/23/2013	3/25/2013	Y	Y	Y
Loan Originator Compensation Requirements Under the Truth in Lending Act (Regulation Z)	CFPB	2/15/2013	6/1/2013	Y	Y	Y
Disclosure of Records and Information	CFPB	2/15/2013	3/18/2013	Y	Y	Y
Disclosures at Automated Teller Machines (Regulation E)	CFPB	3/26/2013	3/26/2013	N/A	Y	Y

Rulemaking	Responsible regulator	Published date	Effective date[a]	Agency stated it conducted analysis required under		
				Regulatory Flexibility Act	Paperwork Reduction Act	Executive Order or statute[b]
Truth in Lending (Regulation Z)	CFPB	3/28/2013	3/28/2013	Y	Y	Y
Final Order in Response to a Petition From Certain Independent System Operators and Regional Transmission Organizations To Exempt Specified Transactions Authorized by a Tariff or Protocol Approved by the Federal Energy Regulatory Commission or the Public Utility Commission of Texas From Certain Provisions of the Commodity Exchange Act Pursuant to the Authority Provided in the Act	CFTC	4/2/2013	4/2/2013	Y	Y	Y
Order Exempting, Pursuant to Authority of the Commodity Exchange Act, Certain Transactions Between Entities Descr bed in the Federal Power Act, and Other Electric Cooperatives	CFTC	4/2/2013	4/2/2013	Y	Y	Y
Definitions of "Predominantly Engaged In Financial Activities" and "Significant" Nonbank Financial Company and Bank Holding Company	FRS	4/5/2013	5/6/2013	Y	Y	N/A
Dual and Multiple Associations of Persons Associated With Swap Dealers, Major Swap Participants and Other Commission Registrants	CFTC	4/8/2013	6/7/2013	Y	Y	Y
Retail Foreign Exchange Transactions (Regulation NN)	FRS	4/9/2013	5/13/2013	Y	Y	N/A
Disclosure of Consumer Complaint Data	CFPB	4/10/2013	3/25/2013	N/A	N/A	N/A
Clearing Exemption for Swaps Between Certain Affiliated Entities	CFTC	4/11/2013	6/10/2013	Y	Y	Y
Identity Theft Red Flags Rules	CFTC and SEC	4/19/2013	5/20/2013	Y	Y	Y
Truth in Lending (Regulation Z)	CFPB	5/3/2013	5/3/2013	Y	Y	Y
Consumer Financial Civil Penalty Fund	CFPB	5/7/2013	5/7/2013	N/A	Y	Y
Amendments to the 2013 Escrows Final Rule under the Truth in Lending Act (Regulation Z)	CFPB	5/23/2013	6/1/2013	Y	Y	Y
Antidisruptive Practices Authority	CFTC	5/28/2013	5/28/2013	N/A	N/A	N/A
Technical Amendments	NCUA	5/31/2013	5/31/2013	Y	Y	N/A
Loan Originator Compensation Requirements Under the Truth in Lending Act (Regulation Z); Prohibition on Financing Credit Insurance Premiums; Delay of Effective Date	CFPB	5/31/2013	6/1/2013	Y	Y	Y

GAO-14-67 Dodd-Frank Regulations

Rulemaking	Responsible regulator	Published date	Effective date[a]	Agency stated it conducted analysis required under		
				Regulatory Flexibility Act	Paperwork Reduction Act	Executive Order or statute[b]
Definition of "Predominantly Engaged in Activities That Are Financial in Nature or Incidental Thereto"	FDIC	6/10/2013	7/10/2013	Y	Y	N/A
Lending Limits	OCC	6/25/2013	6/25/2013	Y	Y	N/A
Retail Foreign Exchange Transactions	SEC	7/16/2013	7/16/2013	Y	Y	Y
Rescission of Supervised Investment Bank Holding Company Rules	SEC	7/18/2013	7/18/2013	N/A	Y	Y

Source: Dodd-Frank Act, *Federal Register*, and other documents from regulators.

[a]To determine our scope for this review, we considered the earliest effective date shown in the final *Federal Register* releases for each Dodd-Frank rulemaking. If the effective date shown fell within our scope, the rule was included even if subsequent rulemakings changed the effective date of the rule.

[b]Executive Order 12,866 requires executive agencies, like the Department of the Treasury, to the extent permitted by law and where applicable, to (1) assess benefits and costs of available regulatory alternatives and (2) include both quantifiable and qualitative measures of benefits and costs in their analysis. Additionally, CFTC, CFPB, and SEC each have requirements for conducting economic analyses of their rules under their own organic statutes. First, CFTC, under section 15(a) of the Commodity Exchange Act, is required to consider the benefits and costs of its action before promulgating a regulation under the Commodity Exchange Act or issuing certain orders. Second, CFPB, under the Consumer Financial Protection Act (Title X of the Dodd-Frank Act), must consider the potential benefits and costs of its rules for consumers and entities that offer or provide consumer financial products and services. Third, under the Securities Act, the Securities Exchange Act, the Investment Advisers Act, and the Investment Company Act, SEC must consider whether a rule will promote efficiency, competition, and capital formation whenever it is engaged in rulemaking and is required to consider or determine whether an action is necessary or appropriate in the public interest. Under the Securities Exchange Act, SEC also must not adopt a rule that would impose a burden on competition not necessary or appropriate in furtherance of the purposes of the act.

[c]This rule is no longer in effect because it was vacated by a decision of the U.S. District Court for the District of Columbia on July 2, 2013. See *American Petroleum Institute et al. v. SEC*, — F.Supp.2d —, 2013 WL 3307114 (D.D.C. 2013).

[d]We did not consider a rule "substantive" for purposes of this report if the agency (1) stated the rule did not require notice and comment; (2) did not conduct analysis of benefits or costs; and (3) concluded, per PRA, that the rule did not impose new information collection requirements or substantively or materially revise existing collections of information.

Note: In this report, we use the terms "rules," "regulations," or "rulemakings" generally to refer to *Federal Register* notices of agency action pursuant to the Dodd-Frank Act, including regulations, interpretive rules, general statements of policy, guidance, and rules that deal with agency organization, procedure, or practice. Combined with our past two reports, we have reviewed all Dodd-Frank Act rules in effect as of July 22, 2013. See GAO, *Dodd-Frank Act Regulations: Implementation Could Benefit from Additional Analyses and Coordination*, GAO-12-151 (Washington, D.C.: Nov. 10, 2011), and *Dodd-Frank Act Regulations: Agencies' Efforts to Analyze and Coordinate Their Rules*, GAO-13-101 (Washington, D.C.: Dec. 18, 2012)

The following table lists the Dodd-Frank rules that we identified as final and effective during the scope period for our November 2012 review—July 22, 2011, through July 23, 2012.

Table 5: Dodd-Frank Rules Effective from July 22, 2011, through July 23, 2012

Rulemaking	Responsible regulator	Effective date	Did regulator identify the rule as having significant economic impact?	Did regulator quantify costs of final rule other than PRA costs?	Did regulator quantify benefits of final rule?	Did regulator qualitatively identify costs of final rule?	Did regulator qualitatively identify benefits of final rule?
Risk-Based Capital Standards: Advanced Capital Adequacy Framework—Basel II; Establishment of a Risk-Based Capital Floor	FDIC, Federal Reserve, and OCC	07/28/11	No	No[a]	No	Yes	Yes
Securities Whistleblower Incentives and Protections	SEC	08/12/11	Yes	No	No	Yes	Yes
Prohibition on the Employment, or Attempted Employment, of Manipulative and Deceptive Devices and Prohibition on Price Manipulation	CFTC	08/15/11	No	No	No	Yes	Yes
Fair Credit Reporting Risk-Based Pricing Regulations	Federal Reserve and Federal Trade Commission	08/15/11	No	No	No	Yes	Yes
Equal Credit Opportunity	Federal Reserve	08/15/11	No	No	No	Yes	Yes
Certain Orderly Liquidation Authority Provisions under Title II of the Dodd-Frank Wall Street Reform and Consumer Protection Act	FDIC	08/15/11	No	No	No	No	Yes

Rulemaking	Responsible regulator	Effective date	Did regulator identify the rule as having significant economic impact?	Did regulator quantify costs of final rule other than PRA costs?	Did regulator quantify benefits of final rule?	Did regulator qualitatively identify costs of final rule?	Did regulator qualitatively identify benefits of final rule?
Public Company Accounting Oversight Board; Order Approving Proposed Board Funding Final Rules for Allocation of the Board's Accounting Support Fee Among Issuers, Brokers, and Dealers, and Other Amendments to the Board's Funding Rules	SEC	08/18/11	N/A	N/A	N/A	N/A	N/A
Authority to Designate Financial Market Utilities (FMU) as Systemically Important	FSOC	08/26/11	No	No	No	Yes	Yes
Family Offices	SEC	08/29/11	Yes	Yes	Yes	Yes	Yes
Security Ratings	SEC	09/02/11; 12/31/12	No	No	No	Yes	Yes
Agricultural Commodity Definition	CFTC	09/12/11	No	No	No	Yes	Yes
Retail Foreign Exchange Transactions; Conforming Changes to Existing Regulations in Response to the Dodd-Frank Wall Street Reform and Consumer Protection Act	CFTC	09/12/11	No	No	No	Yes	Yes
Rules Implementing Amendments to the Investment Advisers Act of 1940	SEC	07/21/11; 09/19/11	Yes	Yes	Yes	Yes	Yes
Privacy of Consumer Financial Information; Conforming Amendments Under Dodd-Frank Act	CFTC	09/20/11	No	No	No	Yes	Yes
Large Trader Reporting for Physical Commodity Swaps	CFTC	09/20/11	No	No	No	Yes	Yes

Rulemaking	Responsible regulator	Effective date	Did regulator identify the rule as having significant economic impact?	Did regulator quantify costs of final rule other than PRA costs?	Did regulator quantify benefits of final rule?	Did regulator qualitatively identify costs of final rule?	Did regulator qualitatively identify benefits of final rule?
Business Affiliate Marketing and Disposal of Consumer Information Rules	CFTC	09/20/11[b]	No	No	No	Yes	Yes
Suspension of the duty to file reports for classes of asset-backed securities	SEC	09/22/11	No	No	No	Yes	Yes
Removing Any Reference to or Reliance on Credit Ratings in Commission Regulations; Proposing Alternatives to the Use of Credit Ratings	CFTC	09/23/11	No	No	No	Yes	Yes
Process for Review of Swaps for Mandatory Clearing	CFTC	09/26/11	No	No	No	Yes	Yes
Provisions Common to Registered Entities	CFTC	09/26/11	No	No	No	Yes	Yes
Debit Card Interchange Fees and Routing	Federal Reserve	10/01/11[b]	Yes	No	No	Yes	Yes
Whistleblower Incentives and Protection	CFTC	10/24/11	Yes	No	No	Yes	Yes
Swap Data Repositories: Registration Standards, Duties and Core Principles	CFTC	10/31/11	Yes	Yes	No	Yes	Yes
Disclosure of Information; Privacy Act Regulations; Notice and Amendments	FDIC	11/14/11	N/A	N/A	N/A	N/A	N/A
Resolution Plans Required	Federal Reserve and FDIC	11/30/11	No	No	No	Yes	Yes
Remittance Transfers	NCUA	11/30/11	No	No	No	No	No
Amendment to July 14, 2011 Order for Swap Regulation	CFTC	12/23/11	No	No	No	No	Yes
Capital Plans	Federal Reserve	12/30/11	No	No	No	Yes	No

Rulemaking	Responsible regulator	Effective date	Did regulator identify the rule as having significant economic impact?	Did regulator quantify costs of final rule other than PRA costs?	Did regulator quantify benefits of final rule?	Did regulator qualitatively identify costs of final rule?	Did regulator qualitatively identify benefits of final rule?
Agricultural Swaps Rule	CFTC	12/31/11	No	No	No	Yes	Yes
Derivatives Clearing Organization General Provisions and Core Principles	CFTC	01/09/12	Yes	Yes	No	Yes	Yes
Position Limits for Futures and Swaps	CFTC	01/17/12	Yes	Yes	No	Yes	Yes
Performance of Registration Functions by National Futures Association with Respect to Swap Dealers and Major Swap Participants	CFTC	01/19/12	N/A	N/A	N/A	N/A	N/A
Mine Safety Disclosure	SEC	01/27/12	No	No	No	Yes	Yes
Reporting Line for the Commission's Inspector General	SEC	02/14/12	N/A	N/A	N/A	N/A	N/A
Investment of Customer Funds and Funds Held in an Account for Foreign Futures and Foreign Options Transactions	CFTC	02/17/12	Yes	No	No	Yes	Yes
Registration of Foreign Boards of Trade	CFTC	02/21/12	No	Yes	No	Yes	Yes
Net Worth Standard for Accredited Investors	SEC	02/27/12	Yes	No	No	Yes	Yes
Real-Time Reporting of Swap Transaction Data	CFTC	03/09/12	Yes	No	No	Yes	Yes
Swap Data Recordkeeping and Reporting Requirements	CFTC	03/13/12	Yes	No	No	Yes	Yes
Registration of Swap Dealers and Major Swap Participants	CFTC	03/19/12	No	Yes	No	Yes	Yes

Rulemaking	Responsible regulator	Effective date	Did regulator identify the rule as having significant economic impact?	Did regulator quantify costs of final rule other than PRA costs?	Did regulator quantify benefits of final rule?	Did regulator qualitatively identify costs of final rule?	Did regulator qualitatively identify benefits of final rule?
Reporting by Investment Advisers to Private Funds and Certain Commodity Pool Operators and Commodity Trading Advisors on Form PF	SEC and CFTC	03/31/12	Yes	No	No	Yes	Yes
Resolution Plans Required for Insured Depository Institutions With $50 Billion or More in Total Assets	FDIC	04/01/12	No	No	No	Yes	Yes
Protection of Cleared Swaps Customer Contracts and Collateral; Conforming Amendments to the Commodity Broker Bankruptcy Provisions	CFTC	04/09/12	Yes	No	No	Yes	Yes
Exemptions for Security-Based Swaps Issued by Certain Clearing Agencies	SEC	04/16/12	No	No	No	Yes	Yes
Business Conduct Standards for Swap Dealers and Major Swap Participants	CFTC	04/17/12	Yes	No	No	Yes	Yes
Commodity Pool Operators and Commodity Trading Advisers: Compliance Obligations	CFTC	04/24/12; 07/02/12	No	Yes	No	Yes	Yes
Authority To Require Supervision and Regulation of Certain Nonbank Financial Companies	FSOC	05/11/12	No	No	No	No	Yes
Implementation of the Freedom of Information Act	FSOC	05/11/12	No	No	No	Yes	No
Investment Advisor Performance Compensation Rule	SEC	05/22/12	Yes	Yes	Yes	Yes	Yes

Rulemaking	Responsible regulator	Effective date	Did regulator identify the rule as having significant economic impact?	Did regulator quantify costs of final rule other than PRA costs?	Did regulator quantify benefits of final rule?	Did regulator qualitatively identify costs of final rule?	Did regulator qualitatively identify benefits of final rule?
Mutual Insurance Holding Company Treated as Insurance Company	FDIC	05/30/12	No	No	No	No	No
Swap Dealer and Major Swap Participant Recordkeeping, Reporting, and Duties Rules; Futures Commission Merchant and Introducing Broker Conflicts of Interest Rules; and Chief Compliance Officer Rules for Swap Dealers, Major Swap Participants, and Futures Commission Merchants	CFTC	06/04/12	Yes	Yes	No	Yes	Yes
Statement of Policy Regarding the Conformance Period for Entities Engaged in Prohibited Proprietary Trading or Private Equity Fund or Hedge Fund Activities	Federal Reserve	06/08/12	N/A	N/A	N/A	N/A	N/A
Commodity Options	CFTC	06/26/12	No	No	No	Yes	Yes
State Official Notification Rule	CFPB	06/29/12	N/A	N/A	N/A	N/A	N/A
Rules Relating to Investigations	CFPB	06/29/12	N/A	N/A	N/A	N/A	N/A
Rules of Practice for Adjudication Proceedings	CFPB	06/29/12	N/A	N/A	N/A	N/A	N/A
Collection of Checks and Other Items by Federal Reserve Banks and Funds Transfers Through Fedwire: Elimination of "As-of Adjustments" and Other Clarifications	Federal Reserve	07/12/12	No	No	No	Yes	Yes

Rulemaking	Responsible regulator	Effective date	Did regulator identify the rule as having significant economic impact?	Did regulator quantify costs of final rule other than PRA costs?	Did regulator quantify benefits of final rule?	Did regulator qualitatively identify costs of final rule?	Did regulator qualitatively identify benefits of final rule?
Assessment of Fees on Large Bank Holding Companies and Nonbank Financial Companies Supervised by the Federal Reserve Board To Cover the Expenses of the Financial Research Fund	Treasury	07/20/12	Yes	Yes	No	Yes	Yes
Supervised Securities Holding Company Registration	Federal Reserve	07/20/12	No	No	No	No	No
Alternatives to the Use of External Credit Ratings in the Regulations of the OCC	OCC	07/21/12; 01/01/13	No	No[a]	No	No	No
Permissible Investments for Federal and State Savings Associations: Corporate Debt Securities	FDIC	07/21/12	No	No	No	Yes	No
Guidance on Due Diligence Requirements for Savings Associations in Determining Whether a Corporate Debt Security Is Eligible for Investment	FDIC	07/21/12	N/A	N/A	N/A	N/A	N/A
Guidance on Due Diligence Requirements in Determining Whether Securities Are Eligible for Investment	OCC	01/01/13[c]	N/A	N/A	N/A	N/A	N/A
Supervisory Guidance on Stress Testing for Banking Organizations With More Than $10 Billion in Total Consolidated Assets	FDIC, Federal Reserve, and OCC	07/23/12	N/A	N/A[a]	N/A	N/A	N/A
Calculation of Maximum Obligation Limitation	FDIC and Treasury	07/23/12	No	No	No	No	No

Rulemaking	Responsible regulator	Effective date	Did regulator identify the rule as having significant economic impact?	Did regulator quantify costs of final rule other than PRA costs?	Did regulator quantify benefits of final rule?	Did regulator qualitatively identify costs of final rule?	Did regulator qualitatively identify benefits of final rule?
Further Definition of "Swap Dealer," "Security-Based Swap Dealer," "Major Swap Participant," "Major Security-Based Swap Participant," and "Eligible Contract Participant"	CFTC and SEC	07/23/12; 12/31/12	Yes	Yes	No	Yes	Yes

Source: GAO summary of information from the *Federal Register*, the Federal Reserve Bank of St. Louis (http //www.stlouisfed.org/regreformrules/final aspx) and Davis Polk & Wardwell LLP.

Note: N/A refers to those rulemakings related to interpretive rules, general statements of policy, and rules that deal with agency organization, procedure, or practice, and thus not subject to Administrative Procedure Act requirements.

[a]OCC undertook an assessment of these rules, which included quantified total cost estimates, but the assessments were not published in the *Federal Register* notices.

[b]Compliance dates vary.

[c]OCC's guidance is included in this review, even though the effective date is outside our scope period, because the accompanying rule and similar FDIC guidance are included in this review.

The following table lists the Dodd-Frank rules that we identified as final and effective during the scope period for our November 2011 review—July 21, 2010, through July 21, 2011.

Table 6: Dodd-Frank Rules Effective as of July 21, 2011

Rulemaking	Responsible regulator	Effective date	Did the regulator have some level of discretion?	Did the regulator identify the rule as having significant economic impact?
Deposit Insurance Regulations; Permanent Increase in Standard Coverage Amount; Advertisement of Membership; International Banking; Foreign Banks (75 Fed. Reg. 49,363)	FDIC	8/13/2010	No	No
Display of Official Sign; Permanent Increase in Standard Maximum Share (75 Fed. Reg. 53,841)	NCUA	9/2/2010	No	No
Internal Controls over Financial Reporting in Exchange Act Periodic Reports (75 Fed. Reg. 57,385)	SEC	9/21/2010	No	No
Commission Guidance Regarding Auditing, Attestation, and Related Professional Practice Standards Related to Brokers and Dealers (75 Fed. Reg. 60,616)	SEC	10/1/2010	N/A	N/A

Rulemaking	Responsible regulator	Effective date	Did the regulator have some level of discretion?	Did the regulator identify the rule as having significant economic impact?
Removal from Regulation FD of the Exemption for Credit Rating Agencies (75 Fed. Reg. 61,050)	SEC	10/4/2010	No	No
Regulation of Off-Exchange Retail Foreign Exchange Transactions and Intermediaries (75 Fed. Reg. 55,410)	CFTC	10/18/2010	Yes	No
Deposit Insurance Regulations: Unlimited Coverage for Noninterest-Bearing Transaction Accounts (75 Fed. Reg. 69,577)	FDIC	12/31/2010	No	No
Designated Reserve Ratio (75 Fed. Reg. 79,286)	FDIC	1/1/2011	Yes	No
Rules of Practice – Handling of Proposed Rule Changes Submitted by Self-Regulatory Organizations (76 Fed. Reg. 4066)	SEC	1/24/2011	N/A	N/A
Deposit Insurance Regulations; Unlimited Coverage for Noninterest-Bearing Transaction Accounts; Inclusion of Interest on Lawyers Trust Accounts (76 Fed. Reg. 4813)	FDIC	1/27/2011	No	No
Issuer Review of Assets in Offerings of Asset-Back Securities (76 Fed. Reg. 4231)	SEC	3/28/2011	Yes	Yes
Disclosure for Asset-Backed Securities Required by Section 943 of the Dodd-Frank Wall Street Reform and Consumer Protection Act (76 Fed. Reg. 4489)	SEC	3/28/2011	Yes	Yes
Conformance Period for Entities Engaged in Prohibited Proprietary Trading or Private Equity Fund or Hedge Fund Activities (76 Fed. Reg. 8265)	Federal Reserve	4/1/2011	Yes	No
Assessments, Large Bank Pricing (76 Fed. Reg. 10,672)	FDIC	4/1/2011	Yes	No
Higher Rate Threshold for Escrow Requirements (76 Fed. Reg. 11,319)	Federal Reserve	4/1/2011	No	No
Shareholder Approval of Executive Compensation and Golden Parachute Compensation (76 Fed. Reg. 6010)	SEC	4/4/2011	Yes	Yes
Establishment of the FDIC Systemic Resolution Advisory Committee (76 Fed. Reg. 25,352)	FDIC	4/28/2011	N/A	N/A
Order Directing Funding for the Governmental Accounting Standards Board (76 Fed. Reg. 28,247)	SEC	5/16/2011	N/A	N/A
Share Insurance and Appendix (76 Fed. Reg. 30,250)	NCUA	6/24/2011	No	No
Modification of Treasury Regulations Pursuant to Section 939A of the Dodd- Frank Wall Street Reform and Consumer Protection Act (76 Fed. Reg. 39,278)	Treasury	7/6/2011	No	No
Retail Foreign Exchange Transactions (76 Fed. Reg. 40,779)	FDIC	7/15/2011	Yes	No

Rulemaking	Responsible regulator	Effective date	Did the regulator have some level of discretion?	Did the regulator identify the rule as having significant economic impact?
Retail Foreign Exchange Transactions (76 Fed. Reg. 41,375)	OCC	7/15/2011	Yes	No
Beneficial Ownership Reporting Requirements and Security-Based Swaps (76 Fed. Reg. 34,579)	SEC	7/16/2011	Yes	No
Prohibition Against Payment of Interest on Demand Deposits (76 Fed. Reg. 42,015)	Federal Reserve	7/21/2011	No	No
List of OTS Regulations to be Enforced by the OCC and FDIC Pursuant to the Dodd-Frank Act (76 Fed. Reg. 39,246)	OCC/FDIC	7/21/2011	N/A	N/A
Office of Thrift Supervision Integration; Dodd-Frank Act Implementation (76 Fed. Reg. 43,549)	OCC	7/21/2011	N/A	N/A
Exemptions for Advisers to Venture Capital Funds, Private Fund Advisers With Less Than $150 Million in Assets Under Management, and Foreign Private Advisers (76 Fed. Reg. 39,646)	SEC	7/21/2011	Yes	No
Consumer Transfer Protection Date (75 Fed. Reg. 57,252)	CFPB	7/21/2011	N/A	N/A
Identification of Enforceable Rules and Orders (76 Fed. Reg. 43,569)	CFPB	7/21/2011	N/A	N/A
Consumer Leasing – Exempt Consumer Credit under Regulation M (75 Fed. Reg. 18,349)	Federal Reserve	7/21/2011	No	No
Truth in Lending – Exempt Consumer Credit under Regulation Z (76 Fed. Reg. 18,354)	Federal Reserve	7/21/2011	No	No
Interest on Deposits; Deposit Insurance Coverage (76 Fed. Reg. 41,392)	FDIC	7/21/2011	No	No

Source: GAO summary of information from the *Federal Register* and Federal Reserve Bank of St. Louis (http://www.stlouisfed.org/regreformrules/final aspx).

Note: N/A refers to those rulemakings related to interpretive rules, general statements of policy, and rules that deal with agency organization, procedure, or practice, and thus not subject to Administrative Procedure Act requirements. In some instances, we found that an agency had discretion to implement the statute, even though the discretion was limited, because the exercise of discretion was important to implementation.

Appendix III: Dodd-Frank Rules Classified as Major, Final as of July 22, 2013

The following table lists the Dodd-Frank rules that have been designated as major by OMB and are final as of July 22, 2013.

Table 7: Dodd-Frank Rules Classified as Major, Final as of July 22, 2013

Rulemaking	Responsible regulator	Published date	Effective date
Issuer Review of Assets in Offerings of Asset-Backed Securities	SEC	1/25/2011	3/28/2011
Disclosure for Asset-Backed Securities	SEC	1/26/2011	3/28/2011
Shareholder Approval of Executive Compensation and Golden Parachute Compensation	SEC	2/2/2011	4/4/2011
Securities Whistleblower Incentives and Protections	SEC	6/13/2011	8/12/2011
Family Offices	SEC	6/29/2011	8/29/2011
Rules Implementing Amendments to the Investment Advisers Act of 1940	SEC	7/19/2011	7/21/2011
Debit Card Interchange Fees and Routing	FRS	7/20/2011	10/1/2011
Whistleblower Incentives and Protection	CFTC	8/25/2011	10/24/2011
Swap Data Repositories: Registration Standards Duties and Core Principles	CFTC	9/1/2011	10/31/2011
Derivatives Clearing Organization General Provisions and Core Principles	CFTC	11/8/2011	1/9/2012
Reporting by Investment Advisers to Private Funds and Certain Commodity Pool Operators and Commodity Trading Advisors on Form PF	CFTC and SEC	11/16/2011	3/31/2012
Positions Limits for Futures and Swaps	CFTC	11/18/2011	1/17/2012
Investment of Customer Funds and Funds Held in and Account for Foreign Futures and Foreign Options Transactions	CFTC	12/19/2011	2/17/2012
Net Worth Standard for Accredited Investors	SEC	12/29/2011	2/27/2012
Real-time Public Reporting of Swap Transaction Data	CFTC	1/9/2012	3/9/2012
Swap Data Recordkeeping and Reporting Requirements	CFTC	1/13/2012	3/13/2012
Protection of Cleared Swaps Customer Contracts and Collateral; Conforming Amendments to the Commodity Broker Bankruptcy Provisions	CFTC	2/7/2012	4/9/2012
Electronic Fund Transfers (Regulation E)	CFPB	2/7/2012	2/7/2013
Business Conduct Standards for Swap Dealers and Major Swap Participants with Counterparties	CFTC	2/17/2012	4/17/2012
Investment Advisor Performance Compensation	SEC	2/22/2012	5/22/2012
Swap Dealer and Major Swap Participant Recordkeeping, Reporting, and Duties Rules; Futures Commission Merchant and Introducing Broker Conflicts of Interest rules; and Chief Compliance Officer Rules for Swap Dealers, Major Swap Participants, and Futures Commission Merchants	CFTC	4/3/2012	6/4/2012
Customer Clearing Documentation, Timing of Acceptance for Clearing, and Clearing Member Risk Management	CFTC	4/9/2012	10/1/2012
Assessment of Fees on Large Bank Holding Companies and Nonbank Financial Companies Supervised by the Federal Reserve Board To Cover the Expenses of the Financial Research Fund	Treasury	5/21/2012	7/20/2012

Rulemaking	Responsible regulator	Published date	Effective date
Further Definition of Swap Dealer, Security-Based Swap Dealer, Major Swap Participant, Major Security-Based Swap Participant, and Eligible Contract Participant Agreement	CFTC and SEC	5/23/2012	7/23/2012
Core Principles and Other Requirements for Designated Contract Markets	CFTC	6/19/2012	8/20/2012
Debit Card Interchange Fees and Routing	FRS	8/3/2012	10/1/2012
Further Definition of Swap, Security-Based Swap and Security-Based Swap Agreement; Mixed Swaps; Security-Based Swap Agreement Recordkeeping	CFTC and SEC	8/13/2012	10/12/2012
Risk-Based Capital Guidelines: Market Risk	OCC, FRS, and FDIC	8/30/2012	1/1/2013
Disclosure of Payments by Resource Extraction Issuers[a]	SEC	9/12/2012	11/13/2012
Conflict Minerals	SEC	9/12/2012	11/13/2012
Ability-to-Repay and Qualified Mortgage Standards Under the Truth in Lending Act (Regulation Z)	CFPB	1/30/2013	1/10/2014
Mortgage Servicing Rules Under the Truth in Lending Act (Regulation Z)	CFPB	2/14/2013	1/10/2014
Mortgage Servicing Rules Under the Real Estate Settlement Procedures Act (Regulation X)	CFPB	2/14/2013	1/10/2014
Loan Originator Compensation Requirements Under the Truth in Lending Act (Regulation Z)	CFPB	2/15/2013	6/1/2013
Clearing Exemption for Swaps Between Certain Affiliated Entities	CFTC	4/11/2013	6/10/2013
Core Principles and Other Requirements for Swap Execution Facilities	CFTC	6/4/2013	8/5/2013

Source: *Federal Register*, GAO's Federal Rules database available at http //www.gao.gov/legal/congressact/congress html.

[a]This rule is no longer in effect because it was vacated by a decision of the U.S. District Court for the District of Columbia on July 2, 2013. See American Petroleum Institute et al. v. SEC, — F.Supp.2d —, 2013 WL 3307114 (D.D.C. 2013).

Appendix IV: Interagency Coordination for Dodd-Frank Rules Effective on July 24, 2012, through July 22, 2013

The following table lists Dodd-Frank rules effective from July 24, 2012 through July 22, 2013 where the issuing regulator(s) coordinated with at least one other federal or foreign regulator during the rulemaking process.

Table 8: Evidence of Interagency Coordination in Dodd-Frank Regulations Effective July 24, 2012, through July 22, 2013

Rulemaking	Responsible regulator	Published date	Effective date*	Coordination required?	Nature of coordination	Voluntary coordination?
Electronic Fund Transfers (Regulation E)	CFPB	2/7/2012	2/7/2013	Y	CFPB consulted or offered to consult with the prudential regulators, the Federal Trade Commission, and Treasury's Financial Crimes Enforcement Network.[a]	N/A
Customer Clearing Documentation, Timing of Acceptance for Clearing, and Clearing Member Risk Management	CFTC	4/9/2012	10/1/2012	N	CFTC coordinated with SEC and the Federal Reserve.	Y
Guidance on the Effective Date of Section 716 of the Dodd-Frank Wall Street Reform and Consumer Protection Act	FDIC, Federal Reserve, and OCC	5/10/2012	7/16/2013	N	Jointly issued guidance	Y
Swap Data Recordkeeping and Reporting Requirements: Pre-Enactment and Transition Swaps	CFTC	6/12/2012	8/13/2012	Y	CFTC coordinated with the Federal Reserve, FDIC, OCC, and SEC.[c]	N/A
Core Principles and Other Requirements for Designated Contract Markets	CFTC	6/19/2012	8/20/2012	Y	CFTC coordinated with SEC.[c]	N/A
Confidential Treatment of Privileged Information	CFPB	7/5/2012	8/6/2012	Unclear	Although unclear about the applicability of Dodd-Frank section 1022(b)(2), to inform the rulemaking more fully, CFPB consulted or offered to consult with the prudential regulators and the Federal Trade Commission.[a]	Unclear

Rulemaking	Responsible regulator	Published date	Effective date*	Coordination required?	Nature of coordination	Voluntary coordination?
Process for Submissions for Review of Security-Based Swaps for Mandatory Clearing and Notice Filing Requirements for Clearing Agencies; Technical Amendments to Rule 19b–4 and Form 19b–4 Applicable to All Self-Regulatory Organizations	SEC	7/13/2012	8/13/2012	Y	SEC consulted with CFTC and the prudential regulators.[b]	N/A
End-User Exception to the Clearing Requirement for Swaps	CFTC	7/19/2012	9/17/2012	Y	CFTC coordinated with SEC.[c]	N/A
Defining Larger Participants of the Consumer Reporting Market	CFPB	7/20/2012	9/30/2012	Unclear	Although unclear about the applicability of Dodd-Frank section 1022(b)(2), to inform the rulemaking more fully, CFPB consulted or offered to consult with the prudential regulators and the Federal Trade Commission. CFPB also requested comments on the final rule from relevant state agencies.[a]	Unclear
Swap Transaction Compliance and Implementation Schedule: Clearing Requirement Under Section 2(h) of the CEA	CFTC	7/30/2012	9/28/2012	Y	CFTC consulted with SEC, prudential regulators, and foreign regulators.[c,d]	N/A
Financial Market Utilities	Federal Reserve	8/2/2012	9/14/2012	Y	The Federal Reserve consulted with FSOC, SEC and CFTC.	N/A
Debit Card Interchange Fees and Routing	Federal Reserve	8/3/2012	10/1/2012	Y	The Federal Reserve consulted with OCC, FDIC, NCUA, the Small Business Administration, and CFPB.	N/A
Further Definition of "Swap," "Security-Based Swap," and "Security-Based Swap Agreement"; Mixed Swaps; Security-Based Swap Agreement Recordkeeping	CFTC and SEC	8/13/2012	10/12/2012	Y	Jointly issued rule.[b,c]	N/A
Electronic Fund Transfers (Regulation E)	CFPB	8/20/2012	2/7/2013	Y	CFPB consulted or offered to consult with the prudential regulators and the Federal Trade Commission.[a]	N/A

Rulemaking	Responsible regulator	Published date	Effective date*	Coordination required?	Nature of coordination	Voluntary coordination?
Registration of Intermediaries	CFTC	8/28/2012	10/29/2012	N	CFTC coordinated with SEC.	Y
Risk-Based Capital Guidelines: Market Risk	FDIC, Federal Reserve, and OCC	8/30/2012	1/1/2013	N	Jointly issued rule	Y
Confirmation, Portfolio Reconciliation, Portfolio Compression, and Swap Trading Relationship Documentation Requirements for Swap Dealers and Major Swap Participants	CFTC	9/11/2012	11/13/2012	Y	CFTC consulted with SEC, Federal Reserve, FDIC, OCC, and foreign regulators including the European Securities and Markets Authority.[c,d]	N/A
Conflict Minerals	SEC	9/12/2012	11/13/2012	N	SEC coordinated with other federal agencies, including the U.S. Department of State, and GAO.	Y
Annual Stress Test	OCC	10/9/2012	10/9/2012	Y	As required by the act, OCC coordinated with the Federal Reserve and FIO. OCC also coordinated with the other banking regulators.	Y
Supervisory and Company-Run Stress Test Requirements for Covered Companies	Federal Reserve	10/12/2012	11/15/2012	Y	The Federal Reserve coordinated with the Federal Insurance Office, FDIC, and OCC.	N/A
Annual Company-Run Stress Test Requirements for Banking Organizations With Total Consolidated Assets Over $10 Billion Other Than Covered Companies	Federal Reserve	10/12/2012	11/15/2012	Y	The Federal Reserve coordinated with the Federal Insurance Office, FDIC, and OCC.	N/A
Annual Stress Test	FDIC	10/15/2012	10/15/2012	Y	As required by the act, FDIC coordinated with the Federal Reserve and the Federal Insurance Office (FIO). FDIC also consulted with the other banking regulators.	Y
Enforcement of Subsidiary and Affiliate Contracts by the FDIC as Receiver of a Covered Financial Company	FDIC	10/16/2012	11/15/2012	Y	FDIC consulted with FSOC.	N/A

Rulemaking	Responsible regulator	Published date	Effective date*	Coordination required?	Nature of coordination	Voluntary coordination?
Swap Data Repositories: Interpretative Statement Regarding the Confidentiality and Indemnification Provisions of the Commodity Exchange Act	CFTC	10/25/2012	10/25/2012	Y	CFTC consulted with foreign regulators.[d]	N/A
Defining Larger Participants of the Consumer Debt Collection Market	CFPB	10/31/2012	1/2/2013	Unclear	Although unclear about the applicability of Dodd-Frank section 1022(b)(2), to inform the rulemaking more fully, CFPB consulted or offered to consult with the prudential regulators, the Department of Education, the Department of Housing and Urban Development, the Federal Housing Finance Agency, and the Federal Trade Commission.[a]	Unclear
Clearing Agency Standards	SEC	11/2/2012	1/2/2013	Y	SEC consulted with the Federal Reserve and FSOC. SEC consulted with other financial regulators as appropriate.	N/A
Determination of Foreign Exchange Swaps and Foreign Exchange Forwards Under the Commodity Exchange Act	Treasury	11/20/2012	11/20/2012	N	Treasury consulted with federal regulators.	Y
Truth in Lending (Regulation Z)	CFPB and Federal Reserve	11/21/2012	1/1/2013	Y	Jointly issued rule.[a]	N/A
Consumer Leasing (Regulation M)	CFPB and Federal Reserve	11/21/2012	1/1/2013	Y	Jointly issued rule.[a]	N/A

Rulemaking	Responsible regulator	Published date	Effective date*	Coordination required?	Nature of coordination	Voluntary coordination?
Delayed Implementation of Certain New Mortgage Disclosures	CFPB	11/23/2012	11/23/2012	Y	CFPB consulted or offered to consult with the prudential regulators, the Department of Housing and Urban Development, and the Federal Trade Commission. CFPB also held discussions with or solicited feedback from the Department of Veterans Affairs, the Farm Credit Administration, the Federal Housing Administration, the Federal Housing Finance Agency, and the Department of Agriculture Rural Housing Service.[a]	N/A
Clearing Requirement Determination Under Section 2(h) of the CEA	CFTC	12/13/2012	2/11/2013	Y	CFTC consulted with SEC, Federal Reserve, FDIC, OCC, and foreign regulators.[c,d]	N/A
Community Reinvestment Act Regulations	FDIC, Federal Reserve, and OCC	12/21/2012	1/1/2013	N	Jointly issued rule	Y
Final Exemptive Order Regarding Compliance with Certain Swap Regulations	CFTC	1/7/2013	12/21/2012	Y	CFTC consulted with SEC and foreign regulators.[c,d]	N/A
Escrow Requirements Under the Truth in Lending Act (Regulation Z)	CFPB	1/22/2013	6/1/2013	Y	CFPB consulted or offered to consult with the prudential regulators, the Department of Housing and Urban Development, and Federal Trade Commission.[a]	N/A
Loan Originator Compensation Requirements Under the Truth in Lending Act (Regulation Z)	CFPB	2/15/2013	6/1/2013	Y	CFPB consulted or offered to consult with the prudential regulators, the Department of Housing and Urban Development, the Federal Housing Finance Agency, and the Federal Trade Commission.[a]	N/A

Rulemaking	Responsible regulator	Published date	Effective date*	Coordination required?	Nature of coordination	Voluntary coordination?
Disclosure of Records and Information	CFPB	2/15/2013	3/18/2013	Unclear	Although unclear about the applicability of Dodd-Frank section 1022(b)(2), to inform the rulemaking more fully, CFPB consulted or offered to consult with the prudential regulators.[a]	Unclear
Disclosures at Automated Teller Machines (Regulation E)	CFPB	3/26/2013	3/26/2013	Unclear	Although unclear about the applicability of Dodd-Frank section 1022(b)(2), to inform the rulemaking more fully, CFPB consulted or offered to consult with the prudential regulators and the Federal Trade Commission.[a]	Unclear
Truth in Lending (Regulation Z)	CFPB	3/28/2013	3/28/2013	Y	CFPB consulted or offered to consult with the prudential regulators and the Federal Trade Commission.[a]	N/A
Final Order in Response to a Petition From Certain Independent System Operators and Regional Transmission Organizations To Exempt Specified Transactions Authorized by a Tariff or Protocol Approved by the Federal Energy Regulatory Commission or the Public Utility Commission of Texas From Certain Provisions of the Commodity Exchange Act Pursuant to the Authority Provided in the Act	CFTC	4/2/2013	4/2/2013	N	CFTC coordinated with the Federal Energy Regulatory Commission and the Public Utility Commission of Texas.	Y
Definitions of "Predominantly Engaged In Financial Activities" and "Significant" Nonbank Financial Company and Bank Holding Company	Federal Reserve	4/5/2013	5/6/2013	N	The Federal Reserve consulted with the other FSOC members and member agencies.	Y
Retail Foreign Exchange Transactions (Regulation NN)	Federal Reserve	4/9/2013	5/13/2013	N	The Federal Reserve consulted with OCC and FDIC and considered CFTC's retail forex rule (adopted on Sep. 10, 2010).	Y

Rulemaking	Responsible regulator	Published date	Effective date*	Coordination required?	Nature of coordination	Voluntary coordination?
Clearing Exemption for Swaps Between Certain Affiliated Entities	CFTC	4/11/2013	6/10/2013	Y	CFTC consulted with FDIC, Federal Reserve, OCC, SEC, and foreign regulators including the European Securities and Markets Authority, European Central Bank, and regulators in the United Kingdom, Japan, Hong Kong, Singapore, Sweden, and Canada.[c,d]	N/A
Identity Theft Red Flags Rules	CFTC and SEC	4/19/2013	5/20/2013	Y	Jointly issued rule	N/A
Truth in Lending (Regulation Z)	CFPB	5/3/2013	5/3/2013	Y	CFPB consulted or offered to consult with the prudential regulators and the Federal Trade Commission.[a]	N/A
Consumer Financial Civil Penalty Fund	CFPB	5/7/2013	5/7/2013	Unclear	Although unclear about the applicability of Dodd-Frank section 1022(b)(2), to inform the rulemaking more fully, CFPB consulted or offered to consult with the prudential regulators and the Federal Trade Commission.[a]	Unclear
Amendments to the 2013 Escrows Final Rule under the Truth in Lending Act (Regulation Z)	CFPB	5/23/2013	6/1/2013	Y	CFPB consulted or offered to consult with the prudential regulators, the Department of Housing and Urban Development, the Federal Housing Finance Agency, the Federal Trade Commission, SEC, and Treasury.[a]	N/A
Antidisruptive practices authority	CFTC	5/28/2013	5/28/2013	Y	CFTC consulted with SEC.[c]	N/A

Rulemaking	Responsible regulator	Published date	Effective date*	Coordination required?	Nature of coordination	Voluntary coordination?
Loan Originator Compensation Requirements Under the Truth in Lending Act (Regulation Z); Prohibition on Financing Credit Insurance Premiums; Delay of Effective Date	CFPB	5/31/2013	6/1/2013	Y	CFPB consulted or offered to consult with the prudential regulators, the Department of Housing and Urban Development, the Federal Housing Finance Agency, the Federal Trade Commission, Treasury, and United States Department of Agriculture.[a]	N/A
Definition of "Predominantly Engaged in Activities That Are Financial in Nature or Incidental Thereto"	FDIC	6/10/2013	7/10/2013	Y	As required by the act, FDIC consulted with Treasury. FDIC also coordinated with the Federal Reserve.	Y

Source: GAO analysis of Dodd-Frank Act, *Federal Register*, and other documents from regulators.

Note: In this report, we use the terms "rules," "regulations," or "rulemakings" generally to refer to *Federal Register* notices of agency action pursuant to the Dodd-Frank Act, including regulations, interpretive rules, general statements of policy, guidance, and rules that deal with agency organization, procedure, or practice. Combined with our past two reports, we have reviewed all Dodd-Frank Act rules in effect as of July 22, 2013. See GAO, Dodd-Frank Act Regulations: Implementation Could Benefit from Additional Analyses and Coordination, GAO-12-151 (Washington, D.C.: Nov. 10, 2011), and Dodd-Frank Act Regulations: Agencies' Efforts to Analyze and Coordinate Their Rules, GAO-13-101 (Washington, D.C.: Dec. 18, 2012).

*To determine our scope for this review, we considered the earliest effective date shown in the final *Federal Register* releases for each Dodd-Frank rulemaking. If the effective date shown fell within our scope, the rule was included even if subsequent rulemakings changed the effective date of the rule.

[a]Section 1022(b)(2)(B) of the Dodd-Frank Act requires CFPB, in prescribing a rule under the federal consumer financial laws, to consult with the appropriate prudential regulators or other federal agencies prior to proposing a rule and during the comment process regarding consistency with prudential, market, or systemic objectives administered by such agencies. Additionally, under section 1015 of the act, CFPB is required to coordinate with SEC, CFTC, the Federal Trade Commission, and other federal agencies and state regulators, as appropriate, to promote consistent regulatory treatment of consumer financial and investment products and services.

[b]According to section 712(a)(2) of the act, SEC shall consult and coordinate to the extent possible with CFTC and the prudential regulators before commencing any rulemaking or issuing an order regarding security-based swaps, security-based swap dealers, major security-based swap participants, security-based swap data repositories, clearing agencies with regard to security-based swaps, persons associated with a security-based swap dealer or major security-based swap participant, eligible contract participants with regard to security-based swaps, or security-based swap execution facilities, for the purposes of assuring regulatory consistency and comparability, to the extent possible.

[c]According to section 712(a)(1), before commencing any rulemaking or issuing an order regarding swaps, swap dealers, major swap participants, swap data repositories, derivative clearing organizations with regard to swaps, persons associated with a swap dealer or major swap participant, eligible contract participants, or swap execution facilities pursuant to Subtitle A of Title 7 of Dodd-Frank, CFTC shall consult and coordinate to the extent possible with SEC and the prudential regulators for the purposes of assuring regulatory consistency and comparability, to the extent possible.

[d]According to section 752(a) of the act, in order to promote effective and consistent global regulation of swaps and security-based swaps, CFTC, SEC, and the prudential regulators, as appropriate, shall

consult and coordinate with foreign regulatory authorities on the establishment of consistent international standards with respect to the regulation (including fees) of swaps, security-based swaps, swap entities, and security-based swap entities and may agree to such information-sharing arrangements as may be deemed to be necessary or appropriate in the public interest or for the protection of investors, swap counterparties, and security-based swap counterparties.

Appendix V: Summary of Rulemakings Related to Selected Dodd-Frank Provisions Applicable to Systemically Important Financial Institutions

The Dodd-Frank Act contains several provisions that apply to nonbank financial companies designated by the Financial Stability Oversight Council for Federal Reserve supervision and enhanced prudential standards (nonbank SIFI) and bank holding companies with $50 billion or more in total consolidated assets (bank SIFI). Table 9 summarizes some of those provisions and the rulemakings, including their status, to implement those provisions.

Table 9: Rulemakings Implementing Selected Dodd-Frank Provisions Applicable to Systemically Important Financial Institutions and Their Status as of November 29, 2013

Dodd-Frank Act provision	Rulemaking status
FSOC designation of Nonbank Financial Companies for Federal Reserve supervision—Section 113 authorizes FSOC to determine that a nonbank financial company shall be subject to enhanced prudential standards and supervision by the Federal Reserve if FSOC determines that (i) material financial distress or (ii) the nature, scope, size, scale, concentration, interconnectedness, or mix of activities at the nonbank financial company could pose a threat to the financial stability of the U.S. FSOC's final rule and interpretative guidance describe the manner in which FSOC intends to apply statutory considerations (related to a six-category framework for size, interconnectedness, substitutability, leverage, and liquidity risk, and maturity mismatch), and the procedures FSOC intends to follow, when making a determination to designate a nonbank financial company for Federal Reserve supervision under section 113 of the act.	FSOC final rule and interpretative guidance 77 Fed. Reg. 21,637 (Apr. 11, 2012) On July 8, 2013, FSOC voted to designate 2 nonbank financial companies for Federal Reserve supervision. On September 19, 2013, FSOC voted to designate a third nonbank financial company for Federal Reserve supervision.
Enhanced supervision and prudential standards—Sections 165 and 166 require the Federal Reserve to impose enhanced prudential standards and early remediation requirements on bank holding companies, including foreign banking organizations with total consolidated assets of $50 billion or more that are treated as bank holding companies for purposes of the Bank Holding Company Act of 1956, and nonbank financial companies designated by FSOC to prevent or mitigate risks to U.S. financial stability.[a] According to the Federal Reserve, the proposed standards for foreign banking organizations and foreign nonbank financial companies supervised by the Federal Reserve are broadly consistent with the standards proposed for large U.S. bank and nonbank SIFIs. The December 2012 proposal includes an additional requirement for certain foreign banking organizations to form a U.S. intermediate holding company, which would generally serve as a U.S. top-tier holding company for the U.S. subsidiaries of the company.	Federal Reserve proposed rules for U.S. and foreign organizations operating in the U.S. 77 Fed. Reg. 594 (Jan. 5, 2012) and 77 Fed. Reg. 76,628 (Dec. 28, 2012), respectively.[b]

Dodd-Frank Act provision	Rulemaking status
Enhanced risk-based capital and leverage requirements required under section 165(b)(1)(A)(i)—capital plans: Bank holding companies with $50 billion or more in total consolidated assets and nonbank financial companies designated by FSOC must comply with the requirements of any regulations adopted by the Federal Reserve on capital plans and stress tests, including the Federal Reserve's capital plan rule, which requires such companies to submit an annual capital plan to the Board for review that, together with the proposed stress tests (below), would demonstrate to the Board that the company has robust, forward-looking capital planning processes that account for their unique risks and permit continued operations during times of stress.[c] Intermediate holding companies of foreign banking organizations would generally be subject to the same U.S. risk-based and leverage capital standards that apply to a U.S. bank holding company. An intermediate holding company of a foreign banking organization with total consolidated assets of $50 billion or more would be subject to the Federal Reserve's capital plan rule.	proposal included in Jan. 5, 2012 rule and Dec. 28, 2012 rule
Enhanced risk-based capital and leverage requirements required under section 165(b)(1)(A)(i)—capital surcharges: The Federal Reserve intends to issue a proposal imposing a quantitative risk-based capital surcharge for all or a subgroup of bank holding companies with $50 billion or more in total consolidated assets, certain foreign banking organizations, and nonbank financial companies designated by FSOC based on the Basel capital surcharge for Globally Systemically Important Banks (G-SIB).[d] The Federal Reserve stated that it may, through a future rulemaking, impose a capital surcharge to an intermediate holding company of a foreign banking organization that is determined to be a domestic systemically important bank, consistent with the Basel Committee's regime or a similar framework.	intention to propose included in Jan. 5, 2012 rule and Dec. 28, 2012 rule
Enhanced liquidity requirements required under section 165(b)(1)(A)(ii)—liquidity risk management standards: Bank holding companies with $50 billion or more in total consolidated assets and nonbank financial companies designated by FSOC would be subject to liquidity risk management standards that require those companies to, among other things, project cash flow needs over various time horizons, stress test the projections at least monthly, determine a liquidity buffer, and maintain a contingency funding plan that identifies potential sources of liquidity strain and alternative sources of funding. Large foreign banking organizations with combined U.S. assets of $50 billion or more must meet liquidity risk management standards that are broadly similar to the standards proposed for U.S. firms.	proposal included in Jan. 5, 2012 rule and Dec. 28, 2012 rule

Dodd-Frank Act provision	Rulemaking status
Enhanced liquidity requirements required under Section 165(b)(1)(A)(ii)—Basel liquidity ratios: The banking agencies have proposed a liquidity coverage ratio requirement, consistent with the international liquidity standards published by the Basel Committee on Banking Supervision for large, internationally active banking organizations with more than $250 billion in assets, nonbank financial companies designated by FSOC for Federal Reserve supervision that do not have substantial insurance activities, and their consolidated subsidiary depository institutions with $10 billion or more in total consolidated assets. The Federal Reserve is proposing a modified liquidity coverage ratio for bank holding companies without significant insurance or commercial operations that have $50 billion or more in total consolidated assets.	Federal Reserve, FDIC, and OCC proposed rule 78 Fed. Reg. 71,818 (Nov. 29, 2013)
Credit exposure reports required under section 165(d)(2): Section 165 also requires the Federal Reserve to impose credit exposure reporting requirements on bank holding companies with $50 billion or more in total consolidated assets, certain foreign banking organizations, and nonbank financial companies designated by FSOC. The joint proposed rule would require those companies to report credit exposures to other covered companies and credit exposures that other covered companies have to that company.	Federal Reserve and FDIC proposed rule 76 Fed. Reg. 22,648 (Apr. 22, 2011)
Concentration limits required under section 165(e): As required by the act, the Federal Reserve would prohibit bank holding companies with $50 billion or more in total consolidated assets, certain large foreign banking organizations and intermediate holding companies, and nonbank financial companies designated by FSOC from having credit exposure to any unaffiliated company that exceeds 25 percent of the company's capital stock and surplus or total consolidated regulatory capital. The Federal Reserve proposed a more stringent credit exposure limit of 10 percent between the largest, more complex financial institutions.	proposal included in January 5, 2012 rule and Dec. 28, 2012 rule
Stress Tests required under section 165(i): Bank holding companies with $50 billion or more in total consolidated assets, certain foreign banking organizations, and nonbank financial companies designated by FSOC are required by the Act to conduct semi-annual company-run stress tests, and the Federal Reserve is required to conduct an annual stress test on each of those companies.[e] The final rule builds on the stress tests required under the capital plans that large, complex bank holding companies submitted to the Federal Reserve for supervision under the Supervisory Capital Assessment Program in 2009, the subsequent Comprehensive Capital and Analysis Review in 2011, and the capital plan rule effective Dec. 30, 2011.	Federal Reserve final rule 77 Fed. Reg. 62,378 (Oct. 12, 2012) for foreign banking organizations, proposal included in Dec. 28, 2012 rule
Resolution plans required under section 165(d)(1): Section 165 also requires the Federal Reserve to require resolution plans from bank holding companies with $50 billion or more in total consolidated assets, certain foreign banking organizations, and nonbank financial companies designated by FSOC. The joint final rule requires each plan to include, among other things, information about the company's ownership structure, core business lines, and critical operations, and a strategic analysis of how the SIFI can be resolved under the U.S. Bankruptcy Code in a way that would not pose systemic risk to the financial system.	Federal Reserve and FDIC final rule 76 Fed. Reg. 67,323 (Nov. 1, 2011)

Dodd-Frank Act provision	Rulemaking status
Debt-to-Equity Limits under section 165(j): Section 165(j) provides that the Federal Reserve must require bank holding companies with $50 billion or more in total consolidated assets, certain foreign banking organizations, and nonbank financial companies designated by FSOC to maintain a debt-to-equity ratios of no more than 15-to-1, upon a determination by the Council that (i) such company poses a grave threat to the financial stability of the United States and (ii) the imposition of such a requirement is necessary to mitigate the risk that the company poses to U.S. financial stability. The proposed rules would implement the debt-to-equity limitation.	proposal included in Jan. 5, 2012 rule and Dec. 28, 2012 rule
Early remediation requirements under section 166: Section 166 requires the Federal Reserve, in consultation with FSOC and FDIC, to prescribe regulations to provide for the early remediation of financial distress of bank holding companies with $50 billion or more in total consolidated assets, certain foreign banking organizations, and nonbank financial companies designated by FSOC. The proposed requirements would include a number of triggers for remediation, including capital levels, stress test results, and risk management weaknesses. In certain situations, the Federal Reserve would impose restrictions on asset growth, acquisitions, capital distributions and executive compensation, and other activities that the Federal Reserve deems appropriate. The proposed rule for foreign banking organizations adapts these requirements to their U.S. operations, tailored to address the risks to U.S. financial stability posed by the U.S. operations of foreign banking organizations and taking into consideration their structure.	proposal included in Jan. 5, 2012 rule and Dec. 28, 2012 rule
FDIC Orderly Liquidation Authority—Title II gives the FDIC new orderly liquidation authority to act as a receiver in the event of a failure of certain systemically important financial companies, including certain bank holding companies and nonbank financial companies that pose significant risk to the financial stability of the U.S. The rule establishes a more comprehensive framework for the implementation of the liquidation authority and is intended to provide greater transparency to the process.	FDIC final rule 76 Fed. Reg. 41,626 (July 15, 2011)
Federal Reserve authority to impose mitigatory actions on certain nonbank financial companies determined to pose a grave threat to financial stability—Section 121(a) allows the Federal Reserve, with a two-thirds vote by FSOC, to impose certain additional restrictions on bank holding companies with $50 billion or more in total consolidated assets and nonbank financial companies designated by FSOC determined to pose a grave threat to the financial stability of the United States, including limiting mergers and acquisitions, requiring the company to terminate activities, or requiring the company to sell or transfer assets or off-balance-sheet items to unaffiliated entities.	No rules issued

Dodd-Frank Act provision	Rulemaking status
Collins Amendment—Section 171(b) requires the appropriate federal banking agencies to establish permanent minimum risk-based capital and leverage floors on insured depository institutions, depository institution holding companies, and nonbank financial companies designated by FSOC. Under the final rule, these institutions must calculate their floors using the minimum risk-based capital and leverage requirements under the prompt corrective action framework implementing section 38 of the Federal Deposit Insurance Act.	Federal Reserve, FDIC, and OCC final rule 76 Fed. Reg. 37,620 (June 28, 2011)
Concentration Limit/ liability cap on large financial institutions—Section 622 establishes, subject to recommendations by FSOC, a financial sector concentration limit that generally prohibits a financial company from merging or consolidating with, acquiring all or substantially all of the assets of, or otherwise acquiring control of, another company if the resulting company's consolidated liabilities would exceed 10 percent of the aggregate consolidated liabilities of all financial companies.	No rules issued

Source: Dodd-Frank Act, *Federal Register*, and other documents from regulators and FSOC.

[a]Section 165 directs the Federal Reserve to impose enhanced prudential standards for bank holding companies with $50 billion or more in total consolidated assets, certain foreign banking organizations, and nonbank financial companies designated by FSOC regarding overall risk management, which were also proposed in the January 5, 2012 rule. Additionally, section 165 also authorizes FSOC to recommend additional enhanced prudential standards for bank holding companies with $50 billion or more in total consolidated assets, certain foreign banking organizations, and nonbank financial companies designated by FSOC to the Federal Reserve.

[b]In this January 5, 2012 proposed rule, the Federal Reserve proposed rules to implement certain but not all of the requirements of sections 165 and 166 of the Dodd-Frank Act and stated its intention to propose others.

[c]Bank SIFIs are already required to comply with the capital plan rule. The Federal Reserve issued its final capital plans rule on December 1, 2011 (see 76 Fed. Reg. 74,631). On September 30, 2013, the Federal Reserve issued an interim final rule that amends the capital plan and stress test rules and clarifies how bank SIFIs must incorporate the new U.S. Basel III-based final capital rules into their capital plan submissions and stress tests. See 78 Fed. Reg. 59,779.

[d]In November 2011, the Financial Stability Board identified 29 G-SIBs and indicated it would update this list annually each November. FSB last updated this list on November 11, 2013. The updated list contains 29 G-SIBs; the same eight U.S. bank SIFIs were designated as G-SIBs in 2011, 2012, and 2013.

[e]Section 165(i)(2) of the Act requires that any bank holding company with more than $10 billion in total consolidated assets and that is regulated by a federal financial regulatory agency also be subject to company-run stress tests. The Federal Reserve issued a separate rule to implement this requirement. 77 Fed. Reg. 62,396 (Oct. 12, 2012).

Appendix VI: Trends in GAO Indicators for Bank SIFIs

As we reported last year, some Dodd-Frank Act provisions and related rules may result in adjustments to the size, interconnectedness, complexity, leverage, or liquidity of systemically important financial institutions (SIFI) over time.[1] We developed indicators to monitor changes in some of these SIFI characteristics. The size and complexity indicators reflect the potential for a single company's financial distress to affect the financial system and economy. The leverage and liquidity indicators reflect a SIFI's resilience to shocks or its vulnerability to financial distress. Like we did in our last report, we continue to focus our analysis on bank SIFIs, given that FSOC only recently designated three nonbank financial firms for Federal Reserve supervision.[2] Our indicators have limitations. For example, the indicators do not identify causal links between changes in SIFI characteristics and the act. Rather, the indicators track changes in the size, complexity, leverage, and liquidity of SIFIs over the period since the Dodd-Frank Act was passed to examine whether the changes are consistent with the act. However, other factors—including the economic downturn, international banking standards agreed upon by the Basel Committee on Banking Supervision (Basel Committee), European debt crisis, and monetary policy actions—also affect bank holding companies and, thus, the indicators.[3] These factors may have a greater effect than the Dodd-Frank Act on SIFIs. As discussed, some rules implementing SIFI-related provisions have not yet been finalized. Thus, trends in our indicators include the effects of these rules only insofar as SIFIs have changed their behavior in response to issued rules and in anticipation of expected rules. In this sense, our indicators provide baselines against which to compare future trends.

---

[1]GAO-13-101.

[2]Our analyses of bank SIFIs include U.S. bank holding companies with total consolidated assets of $50 billion or more and foreign bank organizations' U.S.-based bank holding company subsidiaries that on their own have total consolidated assets of $50 billion or more.

[3]The Basel Committee has agreed on a new set of risk-based capital, leverage, liquidity, and other requirements for banking institutions (Basel III requirements). Additionally, the Financial Stability Board and the Basel Committee have agreed on new capital and other requirements applicable to designated globally systemically important banks (G-SIB requirements). U.S. banking regulators have implemented some of these requirements, and the Federal Reserve has indicated its intention to base some of the SIFI enhanced prudential standards on the Basel III and G-SIB requirements. For more details see appendix V.

SIFI Size

We developed three indicators of size. The first indicator tracks the number of U.S. bank SIFIs. The second indicator measures a SIFI's size based on the total assets on its balance sheet. The third indicator measures the extent to which industry assets are concentrated among the individual SIFIs, reflecting a SIFI's size relative to the size of the industry. A limitation of these indicators is that they do not include an institution's off-balance sheet activities and thus may understate the amount of financial services or intermediation an institution provides. Furthermore, asset size alone is not an accurate determinant of systemic risk, as an institution's systemic risk significance also depends on other factors, such as its complexity and interconnectedness.

As shown in figure 6, there were 33 bank SIFIs (i.e., bank holding companies with $50 billion or more in total consolidated assets) in the second quarter of 2013. The figure also shows that six of the bank SIFIs had more than $500 billion in total consolidated assets (referred to as large bank SIFIs in this report) and were considerably larger than the other bank SIFIs.

Figure 6: 2013 U.S. Bank SIFIs' Total Assets, as of Second Quarter 2013

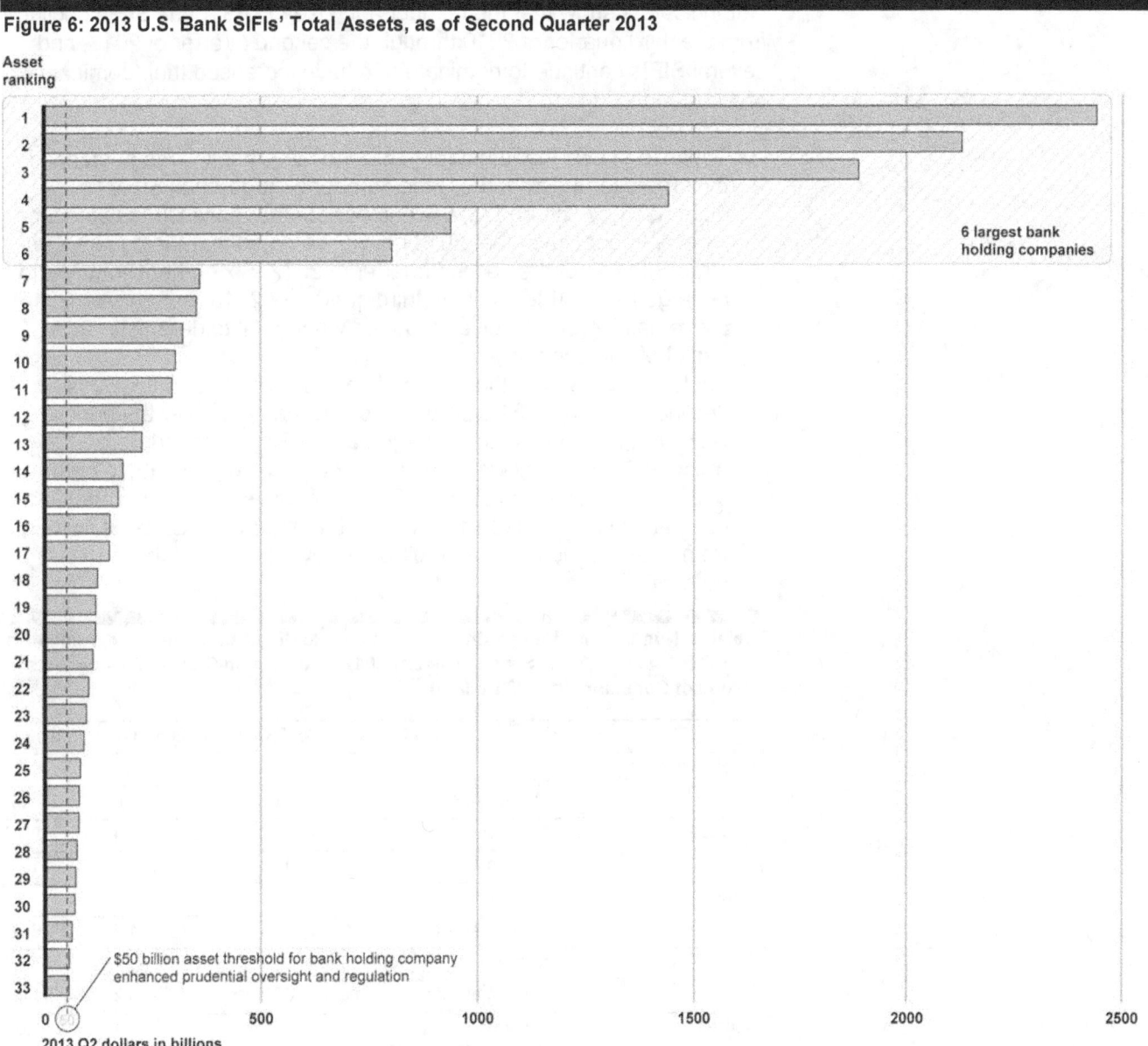

Source: GAO analysis of data from the Federal Reserve Bank of Chicago and the Bureau of Economic Analysis.

Note: Bank SIFIs are bank holding companies with $50 billion or more in total consolidated assets. Bank SIFIs are ranked by assets as of the second quarter of 2013, with 1 being the bank SIFI with the most amount of assets and 33 being the bank SIFI with the least amount of assets.

Our indicators show that the number and size of U.S. bank SIFIs declined from the third quarter of 2010 through the second quarter of 2013, and several SIFIs continue to dominate and have increased their dominance of the market.

- Table 10 shows that the total number of U.S. bank SIFIs decreased by three over the period: (1) the number of large bank SIFIs decreased by one and (2) the number of other bank SIFIs decreased by two. In our November 2012 report, we noted that there were seven large SIFIs as of the second quarter of 2012. Six of them continue to be large bank SIFIs as of the third quarter of 2013. In February 2013, the remaining one received regulatory approval to deregister as a bank holding company.
- Table 10 also shows that the median assets for U.S. bank SIFIs declined by about $21.5 billion (about 12 percent) over the period. However, median assets for large bank SIFIs increased from $1,278.1 billion to $1,662.3 billion, or by $384.2 (about 30 percent), in part because one of the large bank SIFIs deregistered as a bank holding company in 2013. Median assets for the other bank SIFIs decreased from $139.8 billion to $118.8 billion, or by $21 billion (about 15 percent).

Table 10: Number and Median Size of U.S. Bank Holding Companies and Bank SIFIs as of Third Quarter 2010, Second Quarter 2012, and Second Quarter 2013 (Assets in Billions of Constant 2013 Q2 Dollars)

		2010 Q3	2012 Q2	2013 Q2
Total bank holding companies	Number	1,018	1,028	1,035
	Median assets	$1.0	$1.0	$0.9
Total SIFIs	Number	36	34	33
	Median assets	$172.1	$165.6	$150.6
Large SIFIs	Number	7	7	6
	Median assets	$1,278.1	$1,354.6	$1,662.3
Other SIFIs	Number	29	27	27
	Median assets	$139.8	$119.2	$118.8
Non-SIFIs	Number	982	994	1,002
	Median assets	$1.0	$0.9	$0.9

Source: GAO analysis of data from the Federal Reserve Bank of Chicago and the Bureau of Economic Analysis.

Note: Median assets are adjusted for inflation and are measured in billions of constant 2013 Q2 dollars. We used data on top-tier bank holding companies that filed form FR Y-9C, which is generally filed by top-tier bank holding companies with assets of $500 million or more, although a small number of bank holding companies with assets below that threshold also filed form FR Y-9C. We define large bank SIFIs as those with assets of $500 billion or more. Other bank SIFIs are those with assets between $50 billion and $500 billion. Non-SIFI bank holding companies are those with assets less than $50 billion.

- Figure 7 shows that the median market share for large bank SIFIs increased from 7.4 percent to 10.3 percent (or by about 40 percent) of the industry's assets from the third quarter of 2010 through the second quarter of 2013. In contrast, the median market share for the other bank SIFIs declined from 0.8 percent to 0.7 percent (or by about 9 percent) over the same period.

Figure 7: Median Market Share for U.S. Bank Holding Companies by Size, from First Quarter 2006 through Second Quarter 2013

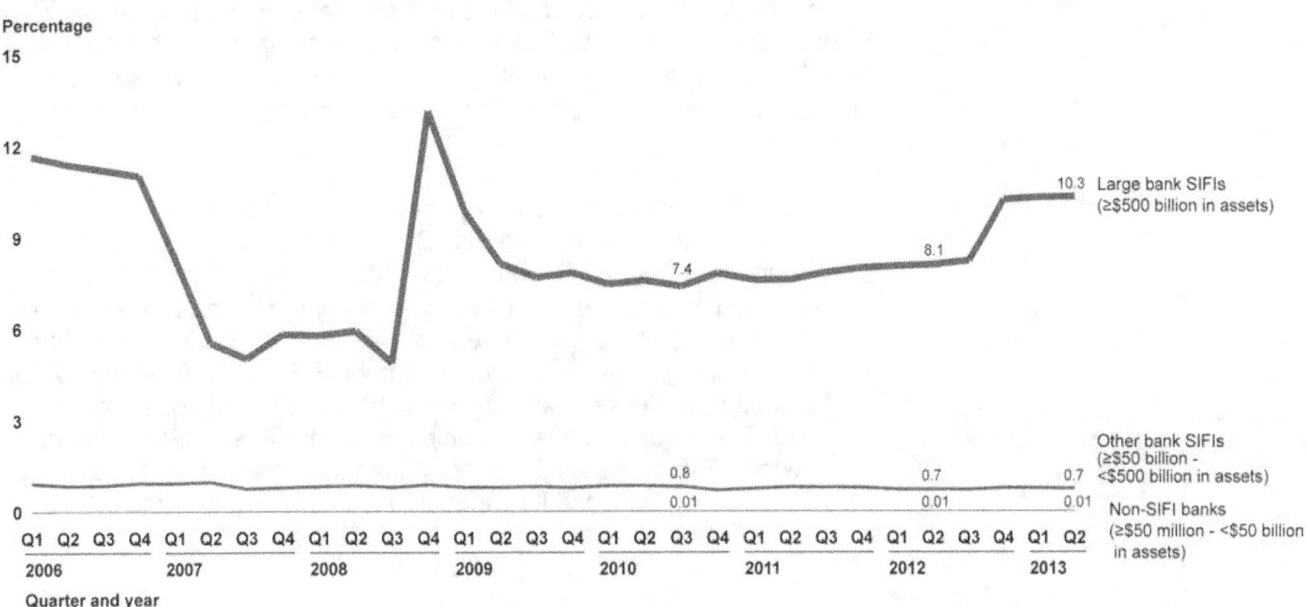

Source: GAO analysis of data from the Federal Reserve Bank of Chicago.

Note: To calculate the median market shares, we calculated the market share for each bank holding company, and then reported the median market share for large bank SIFIs, the median for other bank SIFIs, and the median for non-SIFI banks. We used data on top-tier bank holding companies that filed form FR Y-9C, which is generally filed by top-tier bank holding companies with assets of $500 million or more, although a small number of bank holding companies with assets below that threshold also filed form FR Y-9C. We define large bank SIFIs as those with assets of $500 billion or more. Other bank SIFIs are those with assets between $50 billion and $500 billion. Non-SIFI bank holding companies are those with assets less than $50 billion.

Complexity of SIFIs

Our indicators of complexity are the number of legal entities of bank SIFIs, the percentage of foreign legal entities of large SIFIs, and the number of countries where they are located. An institution's operational complexity may reflect an institution's diverse lines of business and locations in which the institution operates, which are reflected partly through its various legal structures. Consequently, a SIFI with a large number of legal entities—particularly foreign ones operating in different countries under different regulatory regimes—may be more difficult to resolve than a SIFI with fewer legal entities in fewer countries. One limitation of our indicator is that it does not provide information on the relative complexity of SIFIs resulting directly from their various lines of business. Additionally, changes in the operational complexity of a SIFI may be reflected in our indicators only insofar as they result in a change in the number of legal entities.

The complexity indicators continue to show that most large bank SIFIs have a relatively large number of legal entities compared with other U.S. bank SIFIs and that they operate in various countries. They also show that some of the large bank SIFIs may be becoming less but others more complex:

- Figure 8 shows that the six large bank SIFIs in the second quarter of 2013 continue to have more than 2,300 legal entities, with two of them having more than 7,000 and 10,000, respectively.[4] Five of the large SIFIs had fewer legal entities at the end of the second quarter of 2013 than they had at the end of the second quarter of 2010. The median number of legal entities for the large bank SIFIs decreased from 4,991 to 3,682 from the second quarters 2010 to the second quarter of 2013. The median for the remaining 27 bank SIFIs also declined from 108 to 107 over the same period. Within this group, 21 of the 27 bank holding companies had less than 200 legal entities over the period.

---

[4]In our last report we presented the information in figure 3 and table 7 using data as of October 23, 2012, and October 22, 2012, respectively. This report uses data as of the June 30th in 2010, 2012, and 2013 to provide analysis of trend changes that are more consistent with the time frames used in the other indicators.

Figure 8: 2013 U.S. Bank SIFIs' Total Legal Entities, as of June 30, 2010, June 30, 2012, and June 30, 2013

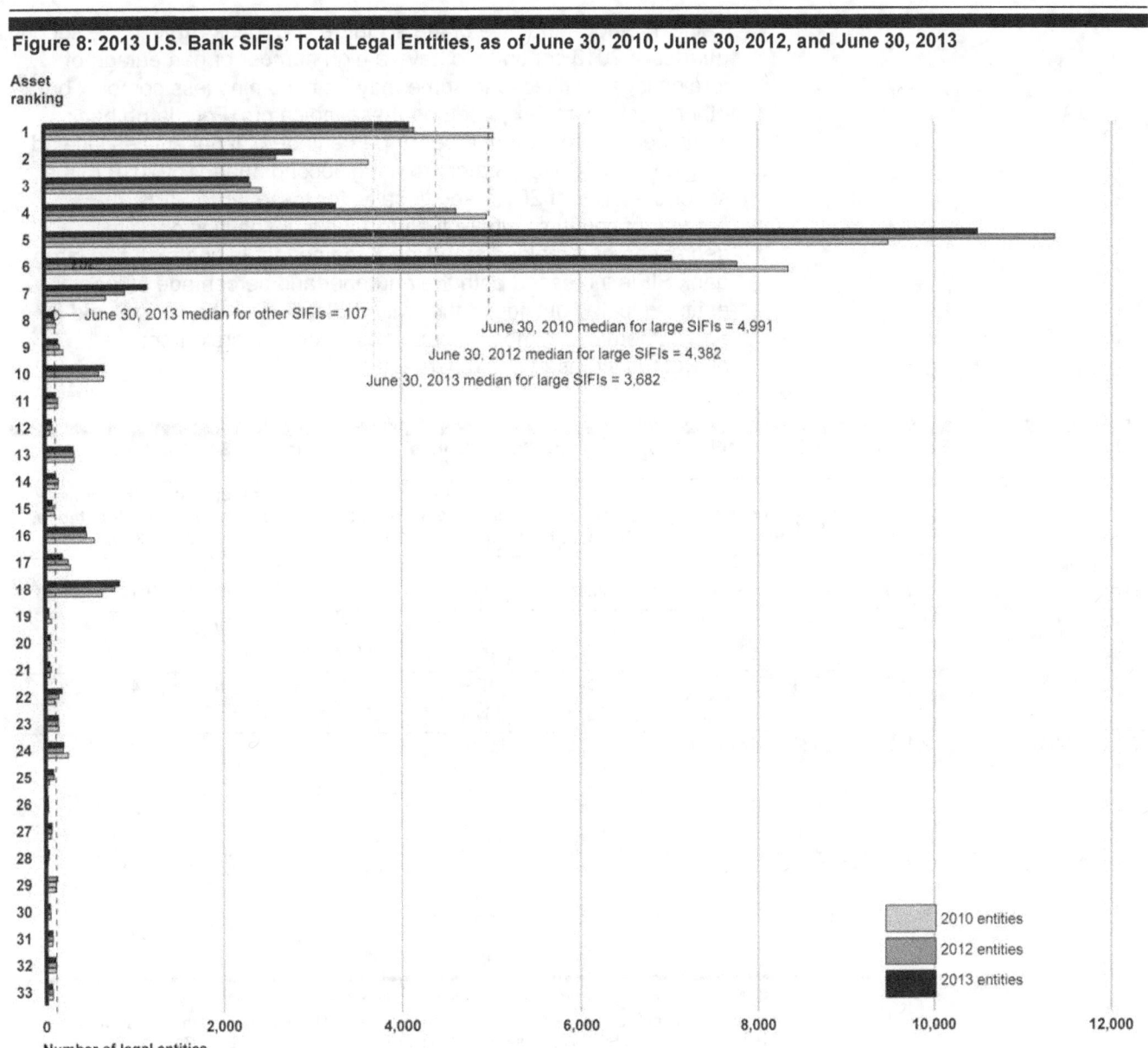

Source: GAO analysis of Federal Reserve Board data from the National Information Center.

Note: Bank SIFIs are ranked by assets as of the second quarter of 2013, with 1 being the bank SIFI with the most assets and 33 being the bank SIFI with the least assets.

- Table 11 shows that five of the six large U.S. bank SIFIs in the second quarter of 2013 continue to have a high number or percentage of foreign legal entities, and some may be becoming less complex but others more complex based on these indicators. Four large bank SIFIs decreased their number or percentage of legal entities located outside of the United States from the second quarter of 2010 to the second quarter of 2013. Additionally, for these large SIFIs, the number of countries where their foreign legal entities operate decreased or remained stable over the period. In contrast, two large bank SIFIs increased both their number and percentage of legal entities located outside of the United States over the period, and for one of them the number of countries where its foreign entities operated increased by 50 percent.

Table 11: 2013 Large Bank SIFIs' Foreign Legal Entities, as of June 30, 2010, June 30, 2012, and June 30, 2013

Bank SIFI ranking	Total number of legal entities, as of June 30th			Number and percentage of foreign legal entities, as of June 30th			Number of countries where foreign entities are located, as of June 30th		
	2013	2012	2010	2013	2012	2010	2013	2012	2010
Bank SIFI 1	4,093	4,159	5,099	798 (19%)	808 (19%)	1,104 (22%)	49	51	49
Bank SIFI 2	2,750	2,604	3,643	1,147 (42%)	669 (26%)	1,014 (28%)	48	47	55
Bank SIFI 3	2,136	2,324	2,449	1,263 (59%)	1,237 (53%)	1,360 (56%)	79	82	83
Bank SIFI 4	3,285	4,621	4,965	187 (6%)	207 (4%)	254 (5%)	21	23	20
Bank SIFI 5	10,635	11,621	9,737	6,041 (57%)	5,986 (52%)	4,244 (44%)	63	61	42
Bank SIFI 6	7,010	7,764	8,425	3,835 (55%)	4,177 (54%)	4,718 (56%)	54	55	59

Source: GAO analysis of National Information Center data maintained by the Federal Reserve.

Note: Foreign entities are entities located outside of the 48 U.S. contiguous states, Alaska, and Hawaii. Large bank SIFIs are those with assets of $500 billion or more. Bank SIFIs are ranked by assets as of the second quarter of 2013, with 1 being the bank SIFI with the most assets.

SIFI Leverage

Although there are many ways to measure leverage, we use two measures: (1) tangible common equity as a percentage of total assets, and (2) tangible common equity as a percentage of risk-weighted assets. The two indicators differ, in part because total risk-weighted assets reflect some of an institution's off-balance sheet activity but total assets do not.

We focus on tangible common equity, because it most closely
approximates the amount of capital available to absorb losses in asset
values in the short term. A limitation of both indicators is that they may not
fully reflect an institution's exposure to risk. Total assets do not reflect an
institution's risk exposure from off-balance sheet activities and generally
treat all assets as equally risky. The calculation of risk-weighted assets is
designed to reflect differences in risk, but the weights assigned to the
assets may not fully reflect the risk exposure associated with those
assets, for example, because assets in broad categories of loans all
receive the same risk weight.

Our indicators suggest that large and other bank SIFIs have decreased
their leverage since the third quarter of 2010, but have slightly decreased
or not changed their leverage levels over the past year.

- Figure 9 shows that median tangible common equity as a percentage
  of total assets generally continued its upward trend for large and other
  bank SIFIs from the third quarter of 2010 through the second quarter
  of 2013. For large bank SIFIs, the indicator increased from 6.3
  percent to 6.8 percent (or by about 8 percent). For the other bank
  SIFIs, the indicator increased from 6.8 percent to 8.2 percent (or by
  about 21 percent).

Figure 9: Median Tangible Common Equity as a Percentage of Total Assets for Bank Holding Companies by Size, from First Quarter 2006 through Second Quarter 2013

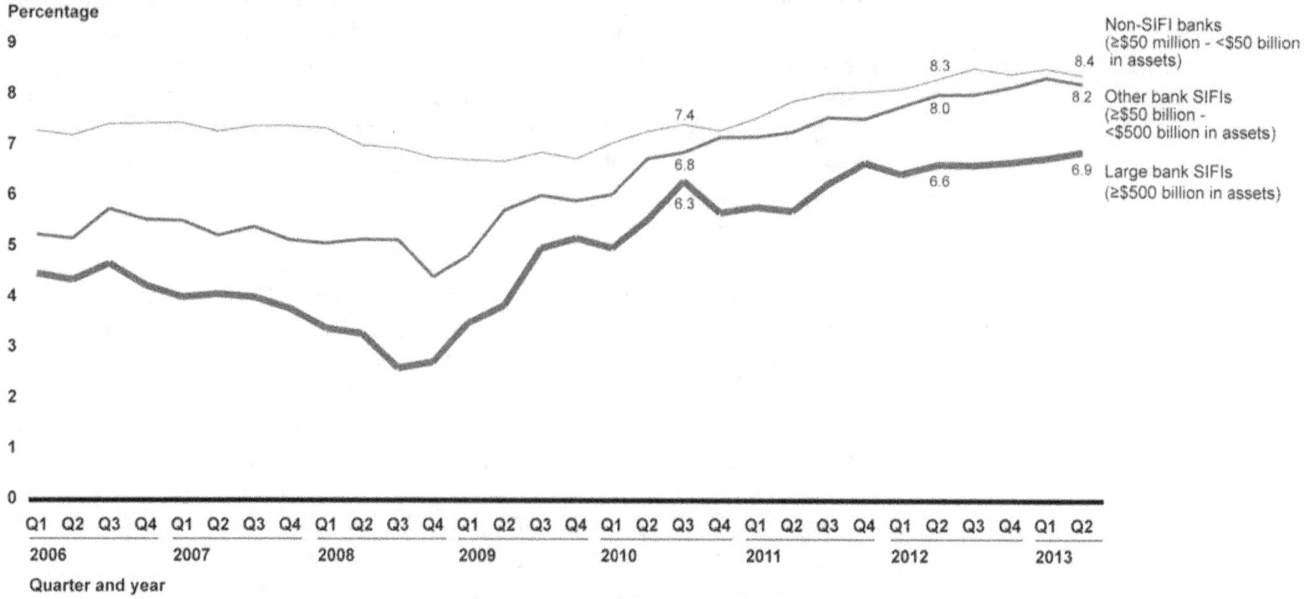

Source: GAO analysis of data from the Federal Reserve Bank of Chicago.

Note: To calculate median tangible common equity as a percentage of assets, we calculated this percentage for each bank holding company, and then reported the median for large bank SIFIs, the median for other bank SIFIs, and the median for non-SIFI banks. We used data on top-tier bank holding companies that filed form FR Y-9C, which is generally filed by top-tier bank holding companies with assets of $500 million or more, although a small number of bank holding companies with assets below that threshold also filed form FR Y-9C. We define large bank SIFIs as those with assets of $500 billion or more. Other bank SIFIs are those with assets between $50 billion and $500 billion. Non-SIFI bank holding companies are those with assets less than $50 billion.

- Figure 10 shows that median tangible common equity as a percentage of risk-weighted assets, which include off-balance sheet activity, increased from the third quarter of 2010 through the second quarter of 2013 but fluctuated over the period. For large bank SIFIs, the indicator increased from 10.8 percent to 11.8 percent (or by about 9 percent) over the period. For the other SIFIs, the indicator increased from 9.4 percent to 10.3 percent (or by about 10 percent) over the period. This measure of leverage did not change much for either group of SIFIs from mid-2012 to mid-2013.

Figure 10: Median Tangible Common Equity as a Percentage of Risk-Weighted Assets for Bank Holding Companies by Size, from First Quarter 2006 through Second Quarter 2013

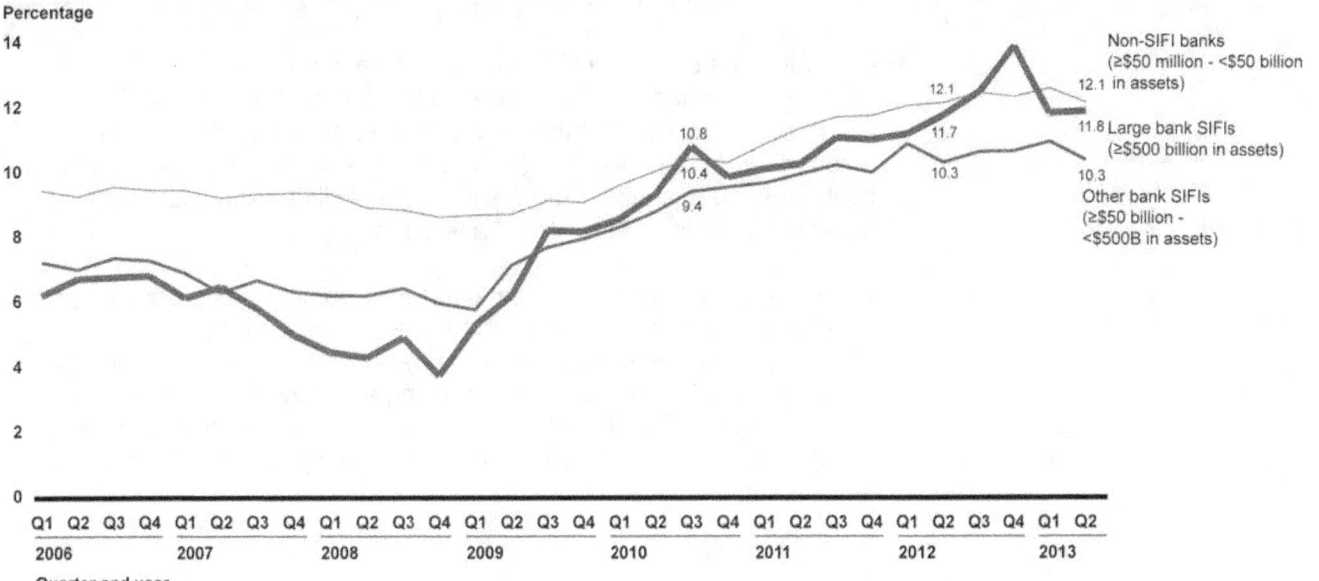

Source: GAO analysis of data from the Federal Reserve Bank of Chicago.

Note: To calculate median tang ble common equity as a percentage of risk-weighted assets, we calculated this percentage for each bank holding company, and then reported the median for large bank SIFIs, the median for other bank SIFIs, and the median for non-SIFI banks. We used data on top-tier bank holding companies that filed form FR Y-9C, which is generally filed by top-tier bank holding companies with assets of $500 million or more, although a small number of bank holding companies with assets below that threshold also filed form FR Y-9C. We define large bank SIFIs as those with assets of $500 billion or more. Other bank SIFIs are those with assets between $50 billion and $500 billion. Non-SIFI bank holding companies are those with assets less than $50 billion.

SIFI Liquidity

We developed two indicators to analyze changes in SIFI liquidity: (1) short-term liabilities as a percentage of total liabilities and (2) liquid assets as a percentage of short-term liabilities. Short-term liabilities are balance sheet obligations due within 1 year; an institution's short-term liabilities as a percentage of total liabilities are a measure of its need for liquidity. Liquid assets can easily be sold without affecting their price and, thus, can be easily converted to cash to cover debts that come due. Accordingly, liquid assets as a percentage of an institution's short-term liabilities are a measure of access to liquidity. For example, if this percentage is under 100 percent, the institution does not have sufficient access to liquidity and is unlikely to have enough liquid assets to cover its short-term debt. A limitation of both of these indicators is that they do not include off-balance sheet liabilities, such as callable derivatives or potential derivatives-related obligations. The second indicator also does not include off-balance sheet liquid assets, such as short-term income from derivative contracts.[5]

Our indicators show that U.S. bank SIFIs have improved their liquidity from the third quarter of 2010 through the second quarter of 2013, although one of our measures shows that large bank SIFIs' liquidity deteriorated from mid-2012 to mid-2013. The figures also show that large bank SIFIs held relatively more short-term liabilities and liquid assets to cover such liabilities than other bank SIFIs.

- Figure 11 shows that median short-term liabilities as a percentage of total liabilities for large bank SIFIs decreased from 55.1 percent to 52.0 percent (or by about 6 percent) over the period, but it increased from mid-2012 to mid-2013, reversing a downward trend. For the other bank SIFIs, the indicator continued its downward trend over the period—declining from 25.4 percent to 20.8 percent (or by about 18 percent).

---

[5]Because these limitations affect both the numerator and the denominator of our indicators, we cannot determine whether the exclusion of off-balance sheet items results in an under- or an overstatement of an institution's liquidity need and access.

Figure 11: Median Short-Term Liabilities as a Percentage of Total Liabilities for U.S. Bank Holding Companies by Size, from First Quarter 2006 through Second Quarter 2013

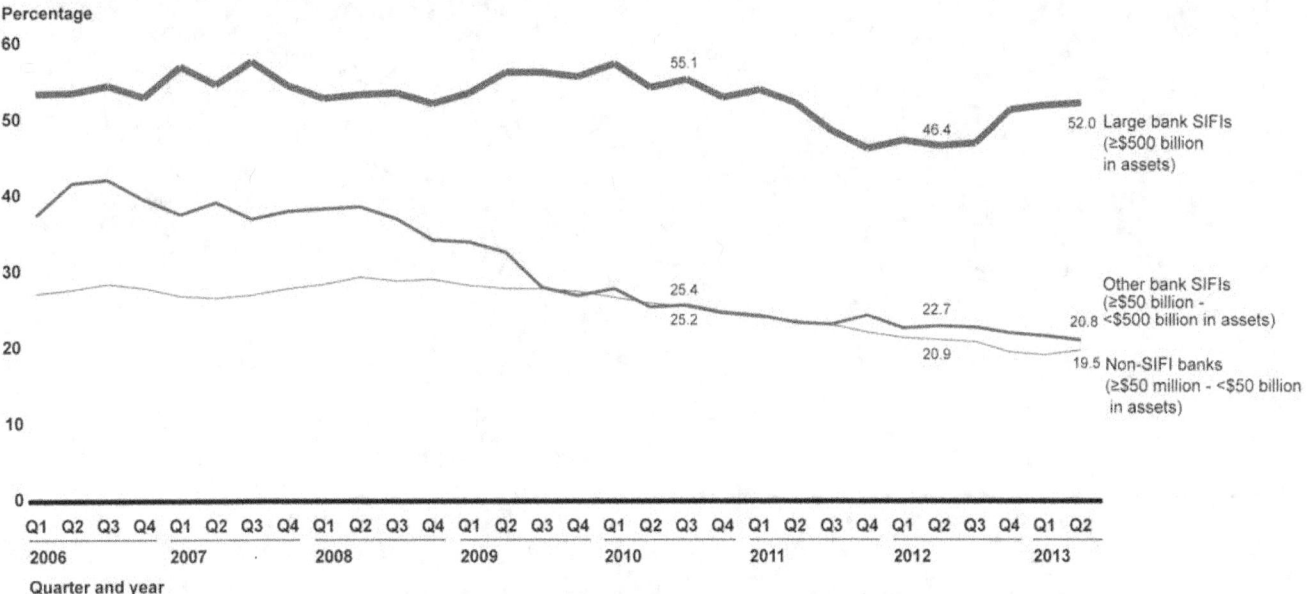

Source: GAO analysis of data from the Federal Reserve Bank of Chicago.

Note: To calculate median short-term liabilities as a percentage of total liabilities, we calculated this percentage for each bank holding company, and then reported the median for large bank SIFIs, the median for other bank SIFIs, and the median for non-SIFI banks. We used data on top-tier bank holding companies that filed form FR Y-9C, which is generally filed by top-tier bank holding companies with assets of $500 million or more, although a small number of bank holding companies with assets below that threshold also filed form FR Y-9C. We define large bank SIFIs as those with assets of $500 billion or more. Other bank SIFIs are those with assets between $50 billion and $500 billion. Non-SIFI bank holding companies are those with assets less than $50 billion.

- Figure 12 shows that median short-term (or liquid) assets as a percentage of short-term liabilities generally continued its upward trend for both large and other SIFIs from the third quarter of 2010 through the second quarter of 2013. Specifically, the indicator increased from 100.7 percent to 136.5 percent (or by 35 percent) for large bank SIFIs and from 79.0 percent to 104.9 percent (or by 33 percent) for other bank SIFIs.

Figure 12: Median Liquid Assets as a Percentage of Short-term Liabilities for U.S. Bank Holding Companies by Size, from First Quarter 2006 through Second Quarter 2013

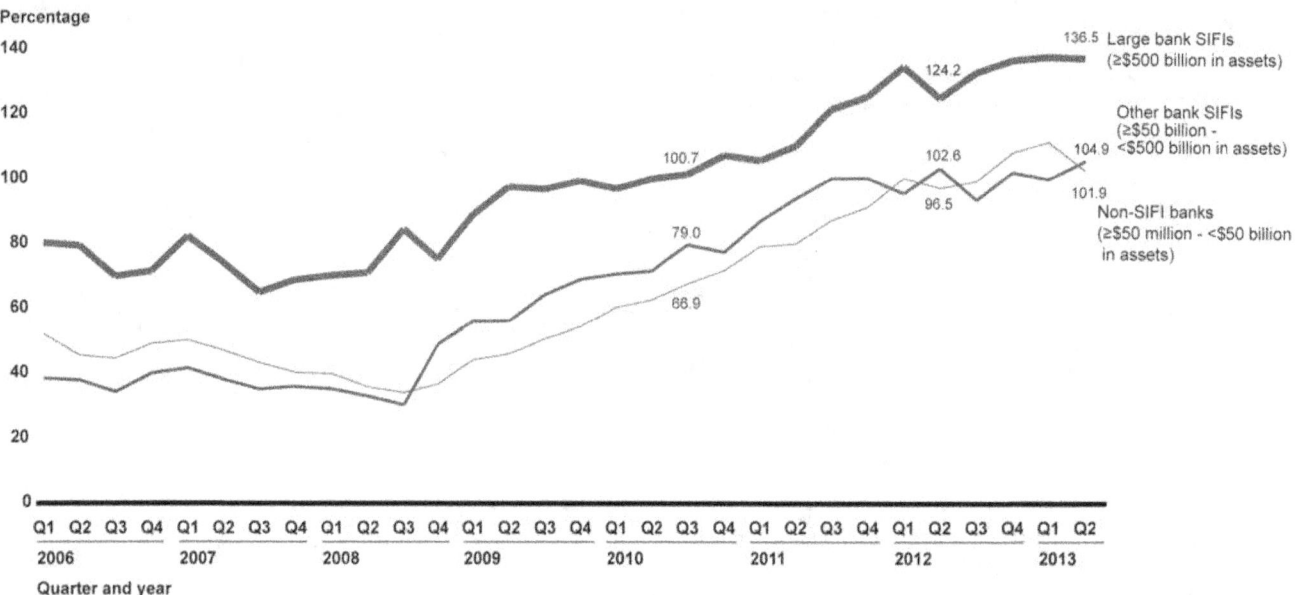

Source: GAO analysis of data from the Federal Reserve Bank of Chicago.

Note: To calculate median liquid assets as a percentage of short-term liabilities, we calculated this percentage for each bank holding company, and then reported the median for large bank SIFIs, the median for other bank SIFIs, and the median for non-SIFI banks. We used data on top-tier bank holding companies that filed form FR Y-9C, which is generally filed by top-tier bank holding companies with assets of $500 million or more, although a small number of bank holding companies with assets below that threshold also filed form FR Y-9C. We define large bank SIFIs as those with assets of $500 billion or more. Other bank SIFIs are those with assets between $50 billion and $500 billion. Non-SIFI bank holding companies are those with assets less than $50 billion.

Appendix VII: Econometric Analyses of the Impact of Enhanced Regulation and Oversight on SIFIs

Methodology

We conducted an econometric analysis to assess the impact of the Dodd-Frank Act's new requirements for bank SIFIs on (1) the cost of credit they provide and (2) their safety and soundness. Our multivariate econometric model uses a difference-in-difference design that exploits the fact that the Dodd-Frank Act subjects bank holding companies with total consolidated assets of $50 billion or more to enhanced regulation by the Federal Reserve but not others, so we can view bank holding companies with total consolidated assets of $50 billion or more (bank SIFIs) as the treatment group and other bank holding companies as the control group. We compared the changes in the characteristics of U.S. bank SIFIs over time to changes in the characteristics of other U.S. bank holding companies over time. All else being equal, the difference in the differences is the initial impact of new requirements for bank SIFIs primarily tied to enhanced regulation and oversight under the Federal Reserve.

Our general regression specification is the following:

$$y_{bq} = \alpha_b + \beta_q + \gamma SIFI_{bq} + X'_{bq}\Phi + \varepsilon_{bq}$$

where b denotes the bank holding company, q denotes the quarter, y_{bq} is the dependent variable, α_b is a bank holding company-specific intercept, β_q is a quarter-specific intercept, $SIFI_{bq}$ is an indicator variable that equals 1 if bank holding company b is a SIFI in quarter q and 0 otherwise, X_{bq} is a list of other independent variables, and ε_{bq} is an error term. We estimated the parameters of the model using quarterly data on top-tier bank holding companies that filed form FR Y-9C for the period from the first quarter of 2006 to the second quarter of 2012.

The parameter of interest is γ, the coefficient on the SIFI indicator, which is equal to one for bank holding companies with consolidated assets of $50 billion or more in the quarters starting with the treatment start date and is equal to zero otherwise. The Dodd-Frank Act was enacted in July 2010, so the treatment start date is the third quarter of 2010. Thus, the parameter γ measures the average difference in the difference in dependent variable between bank SIFIs and other bank holding companies after and before the Dodd-Frank Act was enacted.

We use different dependent variables (y_{bq}) to estimate the initial impacts of the new requirements for SIFIs on the cost of credit provided by bank SIFIs and on various aspects of bank SIFIs' safety and soundness, including capital adequacy, asset quality, earnings, and liquidity.

Appendix VII: Econometric Analyses of the
Impact of Enhanced Regulation and Oversight
on SIFIs

- **Funding cost.** A bank holding company's funding cost is the cost of deposits or liabilities that it then uses to make loans or otherwise acquire assets. More specifically, a bank holding company's funding cost is the interest rate it pays when it borrows funds. All else being equal, the greater a bank holding company's funding cost, the greater the interest rate it charges when it makes loans. We measure funding cost as an institution's interest expense as a percentage of interest-bearing liabilities.
- **Capital adequacy.** Capital absorbs losses, promotes public confidence, helps restrict excessive asset growth, and provides protection to creditors. We use two alternative measures of capital adequacy: tangible common equity as a percentage of total assets and tangible common equity as a percentage of risk-weighted assets.
- **Asset quality.** Asset quality reflects the quantity of existing and potential credit risk associated with the institution's loan and investment portfolios and other assets, as well as off-balance sheet transactions. Asset quality also reflects the ability of management to identify and manage credit risk. We measure asset quality as performing assets as a percentage of total assets, where performing assets are equal to total assets less assets 90 days or more past due and still accruing interest, assets in non-accrual status, and other real estate owned.
- **Earnings.** Earnings are the initial safeguard against the risks of engaging in the banking business and represent the first line of defense against capital depletion that can result from declining asset values. We measure earnings as net income as a percentage of total assets.
- **Liquidity.** Liquidity represents the ability to fund assets and meet obligations as they become due, and liquidity risk is the risk of not being able to obtain funds at a reasonable price within a reasonable time period to meet obligations as they become due. We use two different variables to measure liquidity. The first variable is liquid assets as a percentage of volatile liabilities. This variable is similar in spirit to the liquidity coverage ratio introduced by the Basel Committee on Banking Supervision and measures a bank holding company's capacity to meet its liquidity needs under a significantly severe liquidity stress scenario. We measure liquid assets as the sum of cash and balances due from depository institutions, securities (less pledged securities), federal funds sold and reverse repurchases, and trading assets. We measure volatile liabilities as the sum of federal funds purchased and repurchase agreements, trading liabilities (less derivatives with negative fair value), other borrowed funds, deposits held in foreign offices, and large time deposits held in domestic offices. Large time deposits are defined as time deposits greater than

Appendix VII: Econometric Analyses of the
Impact of Enhanced Regulation and Oversight
on SIFIs

$100,000 prior to March 2010 and as time deposits greater than $250,000 in and after March 2010.

The second liquidity variable is stable liabilities as a percentage of total liabilities. This variable measures the extent to which a bank holding company relies on stable funding sources to finance its assets and activities. This variable is related in spirit to the net stable funding ratio introduced by the Basel Committee on Banking Supervision, which measures the amount of stable funding based on the liquidity characteristics of an institution's assets and activities over a 1 year horizon. We measure stable funding as total liabilities minus volatile liabilities as described earlier.

Finally, we include a limited number of independent variables (Xbq) to control for factors that may differentially affect SIFIs and non-SIFIs in the quarters since the Dodd-Frank Act was enacted. We include these variables to reduce the likelihood that our estimates of the impact of new requirements for SIFIs are reflecting something other than the impact of the Dodd-Frank Act's new requirements for SIFIs.

- **Nontraditional income.** Nontraditional income generally captures income from capital market activities. Bank holding companies with more nontraditional income are likely to have different business models than those with more income from traditional banking activities. Changes in capital markets in the period since the Dodd-Frank Act was enacted may have had a greater effect on bank holding companies with more nontraditional income. If bank SIFIs typically have more nontraditional income than other bank holding companies, then changes in capital markets in the time since the Dodd-Frank Act was enacted may have differentially affected the two groups. We measure nontraditional income as the sum of trading revenue; investment banking, advisory, brokerage, and underwriting fees and commissions; venture capital revenue; insurance commissions and fees; and interest income from trading assets less associated interest expense, and we express nontraditional income as a percentage of operating revenue.
- **Securitization income.** Bank holding companies with more income from securitization are likely to have different business models than those with more income from traditional banking associated with an originate-to-hold strategy for loans. Changes in the market for securitized products in the period since the Dodd-Frank Act was enacted may thus have had a greater effect on bank holding companies with more securitization income. If bank SIFIs typically have more securitization income than other bank holding companies, then changes in the market for securitized products in the time since

Appendix VII: Econometric Analyses of the
Impact of Enhanced Regulation and Oversight
on SIFIs

the Dodd-Frank Act was enacted may have differentially affected the two groups. We measure securitization income as the sum of net servicing fees, net securitization income, and interest and dividend income on mortgage-backed securities minus associated interest expense, and we express securitization as a percentage of operating revenue. Operating revenue is the sum of interest income and noninterest income less interest expense and loan loss provisions.

- **Foreign exposure.** Changes in other countries, such as the sovereign debt crisis in Europe, may have a larger effect on bank holding companies with more foreign exposure. If bank SIFIs typically have more foreign exposure than other bank holding companies, then changes in foreign markets may have differentially affected the two groups. We measure foreign exposure as the sum of foreign debt securities (held-to-maturity and available-for-sale), foreign bank loans, commercial and industrial loans to non-U.S. addresses, and foreign government loans. We express foreign exposure as a percentage of total assets.
- **Size.** We include size because bank SIFIs tend to be larger than other bank holding companies, and market pressures or other forces not otherwise accounted for may have differentially affected large and small bank holding companies in the time since the Dodd-Frank Act was enacted. We measure the size of a bank holding company as the natural logarithm of its total assets.
- **CPP participation.** We control for whether or not a bank holding company participated in the Capital Purchase Program (CPP) component of the Troubled Asset Relief Program (TARP) to differentiate any impact that this program may have had from the impact of the Dodd-Frank Act.

We also conducted several sets of robustness checks:

- We restricted our sample to the set of institutions with assets that are "close" to the $50 billion cutoff for enhanced prudential regulation for bank SIFIs. Specifically, we analyzed two restricted samples of bank holding companies: (1) bank holding companies with assets between $25 billion and $75 billion and (2) bank holding companies with assets between $1 billion and $100 billion.
- We examined different treatment start dates. Specifically, we allowed the Dodd-Frank Act's new requirements for SIFIs to have an impact in 2009 quarter 3, 1 year prior to the passage of the act. We did so to allow for the possibility that institutions began to react to the act's requirements in anticipation of the act being passed.

Appendix VII: Econometric Analyses of the
Impact of Enhanced Regulation and Oversight
on SIFIs

- We analyzed alternative measures of capital adequacy, including equity capital as a percentage of total assets and Tier 1 capital as a percentage of risk-weighted assets.
- We allowed the effect of the treatment to vary by quarter.

Data

We conducted our analysis using quarterly data on bank holding companies that filed form FR Y-9C obtained from the Federal Reserve Bank of Chicago for the period from the first quarter of 2006 to the second quarter of 2013.

Results

Our econometric analysis assesses the initial impact of the Dodd-Frank Act's new requirements for bank SIFIs on (1) the cost of credit they provide and (2) their safety and soundness. Our analysis leverages the Dodd-Frank Act's requirement that bank holding companies with total consolidated assets of $50 billion or more are subject to enhanced regulation by the Federal Reserve but other bank holding companies are not by comparing funding costs, capital adequacy, asset quality, earnings, and liquidity for bank SIFIs and non-SIFI bank holding companies before and after the implementation of the enhanced prudential requirements. All else being equal, the difference in the comparative differences is the inferred effect of the Dodd-Frank Act on bank SIFIs. While some of the SIFI-related rulemakings have yet to be finalized, our estimates are suggestive of the initial effects of the Dodd-Frank Act on bank SIFIs and provide a baseline against which to compare future results.[1]

Our baseline estimates suggest that the Dodd-Frank Act has not been associated with a significant change in U.S. bank SIFIs' funding costs (table 12). To the extent that the cost of credit provided by bank SIFIs is a function of their funding costs, the new requirements for SIFIs are likely to have had little effect on the cost of credit to date.

---

[1]See appendix V for the rulemaking status of the enhanced prudential standards.

Appendix VII: Econometric Analyses of the
Impact of Enhanced Regulation and Oversight
on SIFIs

Table 12: Estimated Changes in U.S. Bank SIFIs' Funding Costs and Measures of Safety and Soundness Associated with the Dodd-Frank Act, from Third Quarter 2010 through Second Quarter 2013

Variable	Measured as	Estimated change (percentage points)			
		Baseline	Sample restricted to BHCs with assets $25-75 billion	Sample restricted to BHCs with assets $1 billion-100 billion	Impact of DFA anticipated enactment by 1 year
Funding cost (cost of credit)	Interest expense as a percentage of interest-bearing liabilities	0.02 (0.02) [0.92]	-0.01 (0.04) [0.88]	-0.02 (0.02) [0.93]	-0.03 (0.02) [0.92]
Capital adequacy (safety and soundness)	Tangible common equity as a percentage of total assets	1.50** (0.22) [0.07]	0.27 (0.69) [0.43]	1.16** (0.24) [0.10]	1.58** (0.24) [0.07]
	Tangible common equity as a percentage of risk-weighted assets	2.02** (0.36) [0.11]	0.17 (0.92) [0.52]	1.12** (0.31) [0.17]	2.21** (0.38) [0.12]
Asset quality (safety and soundness)	Performing assets as a percentage of total assets	0.41** (0.13) [0.30]	1.08 (0.58) [0.72]	0.60** (0.17) [0.34]	0.37** (0.14) [0.30]
Earnings (safety and soundness)	Net income as a percentage of total assets	0.09** (0.03) [0.15]	0.06 (0.12) [0.29]	0.11** (0.05) [0.15]	0.14** (0.03) [0.15]
Liquidity (safety and soundness)	Liquid assets as a percentage of short-term liabilities	-1.80 (8.87) [0.25]	49.23** (15.77) [0.45]	-5.11 (14.56) [0.27]	9.12 (9.23) [0.25]
	Long-term liabilities as a percentage of total liabilities	5.12** (1.01) [0.26]	2.81 (1.65) [0.72]	4.62** (1.77) [0.34]	6.11** (1.03) [0.26]
Number of observations		30,124	478	13,169	30,124
Number of bank holding companies		1,424	31	681	1,424

Source: GAO analysis of data from the Federal Reserve Bank of Chicago.

Notes: We analyzed data for top-tier bank holding companies that filed form FR Y-9C from the first quarter of 2006 through the second quarter of 2013. We estimated the effects of the new SIFI requirements on bank SIFIs by regressing the variables listed in the table on indicators for each bank holding company, indicators for each quarter, indicators for whether a bank holding company is a SIFI for quarters from the third in 2010 through the second in 2013, and other variables controlling for size, foreign exposure, securitization income, other nontraditional income, and participation in the Troubled Asset Relief Program. Estimated changes are the coefficients on the indicators for whether a bank holding company is a SIFI in quarters from the third in 2010 through the second in 2013. We used t-tests to assess whether the coefficient on the SIFI indicator was significant at the 5 percent level. **=estimate is statistically significant at the 5 percent level. Parentheses contain the standard errors of the estimated changes. Square brackets contain the within R-squareds for each regression.

Appendix VII: Econometric Analyses of the
Impact of Enhanced Regulation and Oversight
on SIFIs

Our baseline estimates also suggest that the Dodd-Frank Act is associated with improvements in most measures of U.S. bank SIFIs' safety and soundness. Bank SIFIs appear to be holding more capital than they otherwise would have held in every quarter since the Dodd-Frank Act was enacted (see "Baseline" column in table 12). The quality of assets on the balance sheets of bank SIFIs also seems to have improved since the Dodd-Frank Act was enacted. The act is associated with higher earnings for bank SIFIs in the time period after the act's enactment. It is also associated with improved liquidity as measured by the extent to which a bank holding company is using stable sources of funding. The only measure that has not clearly improved since the act's enactment was liquidity as measured by the capacity of a bank holding company's liquid assets to cover its volatile liabilities. Thus, the Dodd-Frank Act appears to be broadly associated with improvements in most indicators of safety and soundness for U.S. bank SIFIs (relative to non-SIFI bank holding companies).

Our approach allows us to partially differentiate changes in funding costs, capital adequacy, asset quality, earnings, and liquidity associated with the Dodd-Frank Act from changes due to other factors. However, several factors make isolating and measuring the impact of the Dodd-Frank Act's new requirements for SIFIs challenging. The effects of the act cannot be differentiated from the effects of simultaneous changes in economic conditions, such as the pace of the recovery from the recent recession, or regulations, such as those stemming from Basel III, or other changes, such as in credit ratings that differentially may affect bank SIFIs and other bank holding companies. In addition, some of the new requirements for SIFIs have yet to be implemented. Nevertheless, our estimates are suggestive of the initial effects of the Dodd-Frank Act on bank SIFIs and provide a baseline against which to compare future trends.

The results of our robustness checks are as follows:

- Our results for funding costs are generally robust to restricting the set of bank holding companies we analyze to those with assets of $25 billion-$75 billion, but our results for capital adequacy, asset quality, earnings, and liquidity are not.
- Our results are generally robust to restricting the set of bank holding companies we analyze to those with assets of $1 billion-$100 billion.
- Our results are generally robust to starting the treatment in the third quarter of 2009, 1 year prior to the passage of the Dodd-Frank Act. This finding is consistent with the idea that bank holding companies began to change their behavior in anticipation of the act's

Appendix VII: Econometric Analyses of the
Impact of Enhanced Regulation and Oversight
on SIFIs

requirements, perhaps as information about the content of the act became available and the likelihood of its passage increased. However, there may be other explanations, including anticipation of Basel III requirements, reactions to stress tests, and market pressures to improve capital adequacy and liquidity.

- Our results for the impact on capital adequacy are generally similar when we measure capital adequacy using Tier 1 capital as a percentage of assets or risk-weighted assets but not when we measure capital adequacy using equity capital as a percentage of assets (see table 13).

Table 13: Estimated Changes in Bank SIFIs' Capital Adequacy Indicators Associated with the Dodd-Frank Act, from Third Quarter 2010 through Second Quarter 2013

Capital adequacy measured as:	Estimated change (percentage points)
Total bank holding company equity as a percentage of total assets	0.58
	(0.30)
	[0.04]
Tier 1 capital as a percentage of total assets	0.82**
	(0.23)
	[0.04]
Tier 1 capital as a percentage of risk-weighted assets	0.99**
	(0.34)
	[0.10]
Number of observations	30,124
Number of bank holding companies	1,424

Source: GAO analysis of data from the Federal Reserve Bank of Chicago.

Notes: We analyzed data for top-tier bank holding companies that filed form FR Y-9C from the first quarter of 2006 through the second quarter of 2013. We estimated the effects of the new SIFI requirements on bank SIFIs by regressing the variables listed in the table on indicators for each bank holding company, indicators for each quarter, indicators for whether a bank holding company is a SIFI for quarters from the third in 2010 through the second in 2013, and other variables controlling for size, foreign exposure, securitization income, other nontraditional income, and participation in the Troubled Asset Relief Program. Estimated changes are the coefficients on the indicators for whether a bank holding company is a SIFI in quarters from the third in 2010 through the second in 2013. We used t-tests to assess whether the coefficient on the SIFI indicator was significant at the 5 percent level. **=estimate is statistically significant at the 5 percent level. Parentheses contain the standard errors of the estimated changes. Square brackets contain the within R-squareds for each regression.

- Our results are generally robust to allowing the treatment effect to vary by quarter (see table 14).

Appendix VII: Econometric Analyses of the
Impact of Enhanced Regulation and Oversight
on SIFIs

Table 14: Estimated Changes in Bank SIFIs' Funding Cost and Safety and Soundness Indicators Associated with the Dodd-Frank Act, from Third Quarter 2010 through Second Quarter 2013

	Estimated change (percentage points)											
	2010			2011			2012			2013		
	Q3	Q4	Q1	Q2	Q3	Q4	Q1	Q2	Q3	Q4	Q1	Q2
Interest expense as a percentage of interest-bearing liabilities	-0.02 (0.02)	0.01 (0.02)	0.02 (0.02)	0.02 (0.02)	0.01 (0.02)	0.01 (0.02)	0.03 (0.02)	0.04** (0.02)	0.04 (0.02)	0.01 (0.03)	0.04** (0.02)	0.04** (0.02)
Tangble common equity as a percentage of total assets	1.06** (0.20)	1.46** (0.22)	1.46** (0.23)	1.37** (0.23)	1.32** (0.23)	1.43** (0.24)	1.66** (0.22)	1.60** (0.26)	1.52** (0.25)	1.63** (0.26)	1.70** (0.27)	1.89** (0.27)
Tangble common equity as a percentage of risk-weighted assets	1.62** (0.30)	2.14** (0.35)	2.06** (0.37)	1.90** (0.37)	1.81** (0.35)	1.88** (0.40)	2.03** (0.38)	2.09** (0.47)	2.05** (0.46)	2.27** (0.46)	1.98** (0.42)	2.45** (0.42)
Performing assets as a percentage of total assets	0.38** (0.14)	0.45** (0.13)	0.45** (0.14)	0.54** (0.13)	0.52** (0.13)	0.41** (0.14)	0.45** (0.13)	0.46** (0.15)	0.39** (0.15)	0.35** (0.17)	0.29 (0.16)	0.26 (0.16)
Net income as a percentage of total assets	0.13** (0.04)	0.22** (0.05)	0.13** (0.03)	0.12** (0.04)	0.11** (0.04)	0.03 (0.10)	0.05 (0.04)	0.02 (0.03)	0.05 (0.04)	0.10 (0.06)	0.07 (0.05)	-0.06 (0.11)
Liquid assets as a percentage of short-term liabilities	6.34 (6.67)	6.81 (6.89)	-1.83 (7.24)	0.24 (7.60)	4.24 (8.70)	-2.88 (9.71)	-3.52 (11.30)	-3.41 (10.95)	-1.85 (12.09)	-9.86 (12.27)	-14.11 (11.84)	-6.07 (12.02)
Long-term liabilities as a percentage of total liabilities	3.82** (0.87)	3.94** (0.93)	3.36** (1.03)	4.14** (1.02)	5.72** (1.08)	6.13** (1.20)	5.64** (1.24)	5.85** (1.19)	5.85** (1.21)	5.94** (1.23)	5.56** (1.26)	6.15** (1.25)
Number of observations												30,124
Number of bank holding companies												1,424

Source: GAO analysis of data from the Federal Reserve Bank of Chicago.

Notes: We analyzed data for top-tier bank holding companies that filed form FR Y-9C from the first quarter of 2006 through the second quarter of 2013. We estimated the effects of the new SIFI requirements on bank SIFIs by regressing the variables listed in the table on indicators for each bank holding company, indicators for each quarter, indicators for whether a bank holding company is a SIFI in each quarter from the third in 2010 through the second in 2013, and other variables controlling for size, foreign exposure, securitization income, other nontraditional income, and participation in the Troubled Asset Relief Program. Estimated changes are the coefficients on the indicators for whether a bank holding company is a SIFI in quarters from the third in 2010 through the second in 2013. We used t-tests to assess whether the coefficient on the SIFI indicator was significant at the 5 percent level. **=estimate is statistically significant at the 5 percent level. Parentheses contain the standard errors of the estimated changes. Square brackets contain the within R-squareds for each regression.

Appendix VIII: Dodd-Frank Rules Implementing Central Clearing, Capital, and Margin Swap Reforms

The following tables list select Dodd-Frank rules that implement sections of Title VII related to central clearing requirements for swaps and security-based swaps, and margin and capital requirements for swaps entities, as of November 15, 2013.

Table 15: Select Dodd-Frank Rules Implementing Central Clearing Swap Reforms Final as of November 15, 2013

Rulemaking	Responsible regulator	Published date	Effective date
Process for Review of Swaps for Mandatory Clearing	CFTC	7/25/2011	9/26/2011
DCO operations, standards, and risk management	CFTC	11/8/2011	1/9/2012
Derivatives Clearing Organization General Provisions and Core Principles	CFTC	11/8/2011	1/9/2012
Customer Clearing Documentation, Timing of Acceptance for Clearing, and Clearing Member Risk Management	CFTC	4/9/2012	10/1/2012
Process for Submissions for Review of Security-Based Swaps for Mandatory Clearing and Notice Filing Requirements for Clearing Agencies	SEC	7/13/2012	8/13/2012
End-User Exception to the Clearing Requirement for Swaps	CFTC	7/19/2012	9/17/2012
Swap Transaction Compliance and Implementation Schedule: Clearing Requirement under Section 2(h) of the CEA	CFTC	7/30/2012	9/28/2012
Clearing Agency Standards	SEC	11/22/2012	1/2/2013
Clearing Requirement Determination Under Section 2(h) of the CEA	CFTC	12/13/2012	2/11/2013
Clearing Exemption for Swaps Between Certain Affiliated Entities	CFTC	4/11/2013	6/10/2013

Source: GAO analysis of Dodd-Frank Act, *Federal Register* documents.

Note: SEC has not yet proposed rules requiring central clearing for any security-based swap.

Table 16: Select Dodd-Frank Rules Implementing Capital and Margin Swap Reforms Proposed as of November 15, 2013

Rulemaking	Responsible regulator	Rule status	Published date
Margin Requirements for Uncleared Swaps for Swap Dealers and Major Swap Participants	CFTC	Proposed	4/28/2011
Margin and Capital Requirements for Covered Swap Entities	FCA, FDIC, FHFA, FRS, OCC	Proposed	5/11/2011
Capital Requirements of Swap Dealers and Major Swap Participants	CFTC	Proposed	5/12/2011
Swap Transaction Compliance and Implementation Schedule: Trading Documentation and Margining Requirements under Section 4s of the CEA	CFTC	Proposed	9/20/2011
Capital, Margin, and Segregation Requirements for Security-Based Swap Dealers and Major Security-Based Swap Participants and Capital Requirements for Broker-Dealers; Proposed Rule	SEC	Proposed	11/23/2012

Source: GAO analysis of Dodd-Frank Act and *Federal Register* documents.

Appendix IX: Comments from the Financial Stability Oversight Council

DEPARTMENT OF THE TREASURY
WASHINGTON, D.C.

UNDER SECRETARY

November 20, 2013

Ms. A. Nicole Clowers
Director, Financial Markets and Community Investment
Government Accountability Office
441 G St., NW
Washington, D.C. 20548

Dear Ms. Clowers:

I am writing on behalf of Secretary Lew, who serves as the Chairperson of the Financial Stability Oversight Council (Council). We appreciate the opportunity to review the Government Accountability Office's (GAO) draft report GAO-14-67 (the Draft Report) regarding regulatory analysis and coordination to implement the Dodd-Frank Wall Street Reform and Consumer Protection Act (Dodd-Frank Act).

The Draft Report's findings make clear that federal financial regulatory agencies are effectively coordinating and collaborating on the implementation of the Dodd-Frank Act. As the Draft Report notes, these agencies recognize the importance of interagency coordination and have exceeded the coordination and consultation requirements of the Dodd-Frank Act by engaging in numerous instances of voluntary regulatory coordination. These instances generally occurred when a member agency's rules could affect another agency or entities supervised by that other agency, or when the other agency has expertise that could inform the rulemaking. The Draft Report also notes that the Council, or its Chairperson, has fulfilled the coordination or consultative roles for implementation activities required by the Dodd-Frank Act.

The Council has taken a variety of actions to facilitate coordination and consultation among financial regulators. For example, the Council has written protocols for coordination on rules when such action is required under the Dodd-Frank Act. For these and other Dodd-Frank Act rulemakings, the Council's Deputies Committee, composed of senior representatives of the Council's members, and six functional committees, provide forums in which agencies coordinate and consult with each other. The Deputies Committee meets every two weeks to discuss the Council's agenda and coordinate and oversee the work of the functional committees. The results of the Draft Report demonstrate that these efforts have been successful even though Congress did not provide the Council or its Chairperson with authority to require its member agencies to coordinate in all cases. In addition to its ongoing efforts, the Council continually seeks ways to further enhance collaboration through its committees and working groups.

Thank you again for the opportunity to review and comment on the Draft Report. We support
GAO's important oversight function and look forward to working with you in the future.

Sincerely,

Mary J. Miller

Appendix X: Comments from the National Credit Union Administration

 National Credit Union Administration

November 15, 2013

Rich Tsuhara
Assistant Director, Financial Markets and Community Investment
U.S. Government Accountability Office
441 G Street, NW
Washington, D.C. 20548

Dear Mr. Tsuhara:

We reviewed the U.S. General Accountability Office's report entitled *Dodd-Frank Regulations: Agencies Conducted Regulatory Analyses and Coordinated but Could Benefit from Additional Guidance on Major Rules* (GAO-14-67).

We agree with your conclusion that financial regulators, including NCUA, have considerable work underway to implement the requirements of the Dodd-Frank Act reforms that could help improve the U.S. financial system. We also support the primary recommendation the Office of Management and Budget issue additional guidance to help standardize processes for identifying major rules under the Congressional Review Act.

Thank you for the opportunity to comment.

Sincerely,

Mark Treichel
Executive Director

1775 Duke Street - Alexandria, VA 22314-3428 - 703-518-6300

Appendix XI: GAO Contact and Acknowledgments

GAO Contact	A. Nicole Clowers, (202) 512-8678, clowersa@gao.gov
Staff Acknowledgments	In addition to the contact named above, Richard Tsuhara (Assistant Director), Silvia Arbelaez-Ellis, Timothy Bober, William R. Chatlos, Jeremy Conley, Rachel DeMarcus, Courtney LaFountain, Thomas McCool, Marc Molino, Patricia Moye, Barbara Roesmann, and Susan Offutt made key contributions to this report.

GAO's Mission	The Government Accountability Office, the audit, evaluation, and investigative arm of Congress, exists to support Congress in meeting its constitutional responsibilities and to help improve the performance and accountability of the federal government for the American people. GAO examines the use of public funds; evaluates federal programs and policies; and provides analyses, recommendations, and other assistance to help Congress make informed oversight, policy, and funding decisions. GAO's commitment to good government is reflected in its core values of accountability, integrity, and reliability.
Obtaining Copies of GAO Reports and Testimony	The fastest and easiest way to obtain copies of GAO documents at no cost is through GAO's website (http://www.gao.gov). Each weekday afternoon, GAO posts on its website newly released reports, testimony, and correspondence. To have GAO e-mail you a list of newly posted products, go to http://www.gao.gov and select "E-mail Updates."
Order by Phone	The price of each GAO publication reflects GAO's actual cost of production and distribution and depends on the number of pages in the publication and whether the publication is printed in color or black and white. Pricing and ordering information is posted on GAO's website, http://www.gao.gov/ordering.htm. Place orders by calling (202) 512-6000, toll free (866) 801-7077, or TDD (202) 512-2537. Orders may be paid for using American Express, Discover Card, MasterCard, Visa, check, or money order. Call for additional information.
Connect with GAO	Connect with GAO on Facebook, Flickr, Twitter, and YouTube. Subscribe to our RSS Feeds or E-mail Updates. Listen to our Podcasts. Visit GAO on the web at www.gao.gov.
To Report Fraud, Waste, and Abuse in Federal Programs	Contact: Website: http://www.gao.gov/fraudnet/fraudnet.htm E-mail: fraudnet@gao.gov Automated answering system: (800) 424-5454 or (202) 512-7470
Congressional Relations	Katherine Siggerud, Managing Director, siggerudk@gao.gov, (202) 512-4400, U.S. Government Accountability Office, 441 G Street NW, Room 7125, Washington, DC 20548
Public Affairs	Chuck Young, Managing Director, youngc1@gao.gov, (202) 512-4800 U.S. Government Accountability Office, 441 G Street NW, Room 7149 Washington, DC 20548

Please Print on Recycled Paper.

www.ingramcontent.com/pod-product-compliance
Lightning Source LLC
Chambersburg PA
CBHW080255290526
45790CB00005B/1818